TALES AND TRADITIONS

TALES AND TRADITIONS

Readings in Chinese Literature Series

新编中文课外阅读丛书

Volume 2　　FABLES, MYTHS, FESTIVALS, AND MORE

寓言、神话与节日传说

ACTFL Level: Intermediate Mid to Intermediate High

SECOND EDITION

YUN XIAO　　YING WANG　　HUI XIAO　　WENJIE LIU

萧云　　王莹　　肖慧　　刘文洁

CHENG & TSUI

"Bringing Asia to the World"™

CHENG & TSUI

"Bringing Asia to the World"™

Copyright © 2017, 2009 by
Cheng & Tsui Company, Inc.

Second Edition 2017
First Edition 2009

20 19 18 17 16   1 2 3 4 5

ISBN 978-1-62291-116-5 [Second Edition]

The Library of Congress has catalogued the
first edition as:

Xiao, Yun.

    Tales & traditions : for intermediate students /
Yun Xiao ... [et. al].

      p. cm. — (Readings in Chinese literature
      series = [Xin bian Zhong wen ke wai yue
      du cong shu] ; vol. 2)

    Chinese and English.

    Includes index.

    ISBN 978-0-88727-646-0 (pbk.)

    1. Chinese language—Textbooks for foreign
speakers—English. 2. Fables, Chinese—
Adaptations. I. Xiao, Yun. II. Title: Tales and
traditions. III. Series.

PL1129.E5T32 2008
495.1'86421—dc22

                2008062320

Printed in the United States of America

Publisher
JILL CHENG

Editorial Manager
BEN SHRAGGE

Editors
RANDY TELFER, LIJIE QIN

Creative Director
CHRISTIAN SABOGAL

Interior Design
LIZ YATES

Illustrations
KATERINA PAPADAKI

Cover Design
ALLISON FROST

Cover Image
© BELKAG - SHUTTERSTOCK

Cheng & Tsui Company, Inc.
Phone 1-617-988-2400 / 1-800-554-1963
Fax (617) 426-3669
25 West Street
Boston, MA 02111-1213 USA
service@cheng-tsui.com
www.cheng-tsui.com

CONTENTS

目录
目錄

PREFACE TO THE SECOND EDITION

Chinese is the language of the country with the largest population in the world, and in the United States, Chinese is the language of the second largest group of non-English speakers, after only Spanish. To date, although a number of comprehensive Chinese textbooks are currently available in the United States, interesting and informative pleasure-reading materials specifically designed for Chinese learners are scarce at all levels. Learners and instructors of Chinese as a foreign language (CFL) have longed for such materials, and as the first AP® Chinese Language and Culture exam was offered in 2007, the need for quality readings that familiarize students with expressions essential to understanding Chinese culture is now greater than ever.

Tales and Traditions 《新编中文课外阅读丛书》 / 《新編中文課外閱讀叢書》 was created to meet the need for supplementary reading materials for Chinese language learners. Foreign language acquisition research has shown that extensive pleasure reading, in which students read large quantities of level-appropriate books and materials, is essential to attaining fluency in a foreign language. Pleasure reading not only improves students' reading skills, speed, and language proficiency, but also leads them to lifelong fluency and enjoyment of reading in the target language. This series presents stories and anecdotes that are a part of the Chinese literary canon and essential for cultural fluency: sayings from classical philosophers, folk tales, legends, excerpts from great works of literature, and more.

Volume 2 is designed for students who have finished the Novice High to Intermediate Low levels of Chinese study according to the American Council on Teaching Foreign Languages (ACTFL) standards. Its four units, organized by theme, include ten literary adaptations and fables; four legends behind traditional festivals; five fantasies, such as 画龙点睛 / 畫龍點睛 (Dragon Eyes) and 哪吒闹海 / 哪吒鬧海 (Little Nezha Fights the Great Dragon King); and five classical love romances, including 白蛇传 / 白蛇傳 (Lady White Snake) and 梁山伯与祝英台 / 梁山伯與祝英台 (The Story of Two Butterfly Lovers). Material within each unit increases in difficulty, but students and teachers should feel comfortable reading the selections in any order.

Each story in this series has an interesting plotline, a vocabulary list, and stimulating post-reading questions. The stories can be used for individual student reading and/or instructor-facilitated classroom reading. Using the discussion questions, teachers can engage students in comprehension checks, cross-cultural comparisons, and real-life reflections. Students may also enjoy acting out the stories (see the "Teaching Note" at the end of this Preface for more information). Teachers will find the stories easy to use and an essential tool to improve learners' presentation skills. They will help students gain literacy and familiarity with Chinese written texts that are at the heart of Chinese culture. This focus on reading comprehension and cultural knowledge makes the *Tales and Traditions* series an excellent companion for students who are preparing for the AP® Chinese Language and Culture exam, or other standardized tests.

A comprehensive index of all vocabulary words in the volume, arranged in alphabetical order by *pinyin*, will help students review and look up unfamiliar words. Personal names that appear in the stories are underlined, so that students can easily recognize and identify them.

About the *Tales and Traditions* Series
Differentiated in the use of characters, phrases, sentence patterns, and discourse features, the series consists of four volumes corresponding to the Intermediate Low/Mid, Intermediate Mid/

High, Intermediate High/Advanced Low, and Advanced Low/Mid ACTFL levels, respectively. All stories are adapted to a level appropriate for learners of Chinese, from the Intermediate Low/Mid level in Volume 1 to the Advanced Low/Mid level in Volume 4. Each volume features a variety of genres, such as myths, legends, classical and popular short stories, fables, Tang/Song poems, satirical and amusing essays and stories, and extracts from well-known literature. All the stories are illustrated to engage the reader and aid comprehension. Authentic passages, vocabulary words, and sentence patterns have been adapted to keep the stories level-appropriate, while maintaining their originality.

In each volume, vocabulary words, forms of usage, idioms, expressions, sentence patterns, and phrases are selected according to their frequency of use and expository requirements. Students should focus on reading for comprehension, rather than being able to recognize each and every character. For Intermediate Low/Mid students' ease of vocabulary reference, however, an appendix of texts in *pinyin* is included in Volume 1 so that they can quickly check the pronunciation of a word and look it up in the index or a dictionary.

To adapt these stories and compile vocabulary lists, we used three main sources: *Xiandai Hanyu Pinlu Cidian* (现代汉语频率词典 / 現代漢語頻率詞典) (1986), *Hanyu Shuiping Dengji Biaozhun he Dengji Dagang* (汉语水平等级标准和等级大纲 / 漢語水平等級標準和等級大綱) (1988), and *Far East 3000 Chinese Character Dictionary* (远东汉字三千字典 / 遠東漢字三千字典) (2003). Words and phrases used in the first three volumes are selected in accordance with the 甲 乙 丙 levels specified in 漢語水平等級標準和等級大綱. The length (i.e., the number of running characters) of the stories gradually increases as the academic level advances, from 150 to 1,000 characters per story for Volumes 1 and 2, and from 500 to 2,000 characters per story for Volumes 3 and 4. For the first two volumes, most characters were selected from the first 1,500 most frequently used words listed in 現代漢語頻率詞典, which are recycled and expanded to the first 3,500 words and beyond in the final two volumes.

As globalization, multiculturalism, and multilingualism change the way people interact with one another around the globe, a high level of Chinese language proficiency has become an important qualification for individuals in the United States and other countries to gain a competitive advantage in academics, business, and other areas. We hope this series of stories will help students become fluent readers and speakers of Chinese, as well as global citizens with a multicultural perspective.

What's New in the Second Edition?

Discussion questions in the new edition of *Tales and Traditions* have been revised to better prepare students for the reading comprehension questions on the AP® Exam in Chinese Language and Culture. The layout of the text is now easier to read. Background information about historical figures has been added before related stories.

TEACHING NOTE

For teachers and students who are using this book as supplementary reading for a Chinese course, we have provided questions to stimulate class discussions of the stories in both Chinese and English. In addition, students can be asked to retell the stories in their own words when class time allows. For extra speaking practice, students may enjoy acting out the stories in small groups. Each group selects a story, writes speaking lines, and assigns roles. A special day or two can be set aside at mid-term or semester's end for performance of the plays.

ABBREVIATIONS OF PARTS OF SPEECH

ABBREVIATION	PART OF SPEECH
adj.	Adjective
adv.	Adverb
av.	Auxiliary verb
ce.	Common expression
conj.	Conjunction
mw.	Measure word
n.	Noun
np.	Noun phrase
on.	Onomatopoeic word
part.	Particle
pn.	Proper noun
v.	Verb
vc.	Verb plus complement
vo.	Verb plus object

I

Fables and Literary Adaptations
第一章 寓言典故
第一章 寓言典故

1

The Man from the State of Zheng Who Needed New Shoes

郑人买履[1*]
鄭人買履[1]

Zhèng rén mǎi lǚ

*Note: Vocabulary words are numbered within the stories for easy reference.

很久以前，有一个郑国人。他的家住在一个离集市₂很远的地方，买东西很不方便。而且这个集市不是每天都开，要好几天才开一次。所以，他每次去集市以前，都要写下要买的东西，这样才不会忘记₃。

有一天，这个郑国人的鞋子破了，他打算去集市买一双新的。他先用一根小绳子把自己的脚量了一下，然后把小绳子收起来。他想："过几天，我到集市上去，就按照₄这根绳子的尺寸₅去买新鞋子。"

几天过去了，这个郑国人的鞋子越来越破了。到了集市那一天，他很早就起了床，急急忙忙地往集市跑去。

集市上人很多，但是他很快就找到了卖鞋子的地方。他挑₆了半天，才挑到了一双自己喜欢的鞋子。他正要给钱，忽然₇想起了绳子。

很久以前，有一個鄭國人。他的家住在一個離集市₂很遠的地方，買東西很不方便。而且這個集市不是每天都開，要好幾天才開一次。所以，他每次去集市以前，都要寫下要買的東西，這樣才不會忘記₃。

有一天，這個鄭國人的鞋子破了，他打算去集市買一雙新的。他先用一根小繩子把自己的腳量了一下，然後把小繩子收起來。他想："過幾天，我到集市上去，就按照₄這根繩子的尺寸₅去買新鞋子。"

幾天過去了，這個鄭國人的鞋子越來越破了。到了集市那一天，他很早就起了床，急急忙忙地往集市跑去。

集市上人很多，但是他很快就找到了賣鞋子的地方。他挑₆了半天，才挑到了一雙自己喜歡的鞋子。他正要給錢，忽然₇想起了繩子。他要用那根繩子來量一下新鞋子，

他要用那根绳子来量一下新鞋子，看看合适不合适。可是他找啊找啊，找了半天，也没有找到那根绳子。他不好意思地[8]对卖鞋子的人说："对不起，我忘了带尺寸了。请你等一下，我回家去找，找到以后，我再回来。"说完，他就往家里跑。

等他回家找到了绳子，再跑回集市的时候，卖鞋的人已经走了，集市也散[9]了。旁边的人看见他很不高兴，就问他："你是给谁买鞋子啊？"他说："给我自己。"大家都觉得很奇怪，问他说："你刚才[10]不是挑好了一双吗？为什么不买呢？"他回答说："我忘了带尺寸了，就回家去找。可是我家住得很远，等找到了再跑回来，卖鞋子的人已经走了。"集上的人都说："你给你自己买鞋，就用自己的脚量一下，穿上看看就行了，为什么要跑回去找尺寸呢？"这个人说："买鞋子当然要尺寸啦！要不然，怎么能知道脚有多长呢？"大家听了，都笑起来了："你那个尺寸是怎么来的呢？不就是从你自己的脚上量下来的吗？"

这个人跑来跑去，忙了一天，新鞋没有买到，脚上的鞋子也破得不能再穿了。

看看合適不合適。可是他找啊找啊，找了半天，也沒有找到那根繩子。他不好意思地[8]對賣鞋子的人說："對不起，我忘了帶尺寸了。請你等一下，我回家去找，找到以後，我再回來。"說完，他就往家裡跑。

　　等他回家找到了繩子，再跑回集市的時候，賣鞋的人已經走了，集市也散[9]了。旁邊的人看見他很不高興，就問他："你是給誰買鞋子啊？"他說："給我自己。"大家都覺得很奇怪，問他說："你剛才[10]不是挑好了一雙嗎？為什麼不買呢？"他回答說："我忘了帶尺寸了，就回家去找。可是我家住得很遠，等找到了再跑回來，賣鞋子的人已經走了。"集上的人都說："你給你自己買鞋，就用自己的腳量一下，穿上看看就行了，為什麼要跑回去找尺寸呢？"這個人說："買鞋子當然要尺寸啦！要不然，怎麼能知道腳有多長呢？"大家聽了，都笑起來了："你那個尺寸是怎麼來的呢？不就是從你自己的腳上量下來的嗎？"

　　這個人跑來跑去，忙了一天，新鞋沒有買到，腳上的鞋子也破得不能再穿了。

Vocabulary List

	SIMPLIFIED CHARACTERS	TRADITIONAL CHARACTERS	PINYIN	PART OF SPEECH	ENGLISH DEFINITION
1	郑(国)人	鄭(國)人	Zhèng(guó) rén	n.	a person from the state of Zheng
	履	履	lǚ	n.	shoes
2	集市	集市	jíshì	n.	marketplace
3	忘记	忘記	wàngjì	v.	to forget
4	按照	按照	ànzhào	prep.	according to
5	尺寸	尺寸	chǐcùn	n.	size, measurement (lit. foot and inch)
6	挑	挑	tiāo	v.	to select, to choose
7	忽然	忽然	hūrán	adv.	suddenly
8	不好意思地	不好意思地	bùhǎo yìsi de	adv.	embarrassedly
9	散	散	sàn	v.	to disperse, to scatter
10	刚才	剛才	gāngcái	adv.	minutes ago, just now

Questions

1 The man from Zheng used his string to

A. measure the distance from his house to the market.

B. measure his feet.

C. tie his shoes.

D. tie his shoes to his belt.

2 What happened the first time the man went to the market?

A. He measured his feet with his measuring string.

B. He found a pair of shoes he liked.

C. He could not find a shoe merchant.

D. He was too tired to buy shoes.

3 Why did the man rush home before buying a pair of shoes?

A. He forgot to bring money with him.

B. He realized he left his house without locking the door.

C. He forgot to bring his measuring string.

D. He realized he already bought a new pair of shoes.

4 What happened when the man returned to the market?

A. The merchant had already sold the pair of shoes he wanted.

B. He could not find the pair of shoes he wanted.

C. He could not find his measuring string.

D. The merchant had already left and closed shop.

5 Why was the man laughed at?

A. His shoes were untied the whole time.

B. He didn't need a measuring string to buy a pair of shoes.

C. His shoes fell apart when he ran back to the market.

D. He didn't have the correct measurement of his feet.

6 After a day of running back and forth, the man ultimately

A. bought a pair of shoes that fit him.

B. received a pair of shoes from a sympathetic onlooker.

C. fixed the holes in his old shoes.

D. returned home without buying any new shoes.

7 Which sentence best describes the moral of this story?

A. Never begin a task without properly preparing first.

B. Only qualified people should take measurements.

C. It is better to be flexible than to strictly adhere to set ideas.

D. A wise person takes good care of his/her shoes.

DISCUSSION	2. How does this story demonstrate irony?
1. Online, research the state of Zheng. When did the state of Zheng exist? In roughly what part of modern China was it located?	3. Do you know any other Chinese stories that you could tell the man from Zheng as advice? If not, refer to the story called "Cao Chong Weighs an Elephant" (曹冲称象 / 曹沖稱象) in *Tales and Traditions*, Volume 1 or read about it online. How might the message of this or another story help the man from Zheng?

2

Suspecting His Neighbor of Stealing an Ax

疑邻盗斧₁
疑鄰盜斧₁

Yí lín dào fǔ

从前，有一个人以砍柴[2]为生[3]。有一天他上山去砍柴，回家以后，发现斧子不见了。他找啊找啊，在家里到处找，找了好几遍，怎么也找不到。

这个人想，斧子到哪儿去了呢？可是怎么也想不起来。这时，他看见自己的邻居从门前走过。不知道为什么，他觉得邻居看起来有点慌张[4]，好像跟平常不一样。他想：对了，一定是邻居把我的斧子偷走了！

这个人越想越觉得自己的怀疑很对，他就开始悄悄地[5]观察[6]他的邻居。越观察他越觉得是邻居偷了他的斧子。因为没有证据[7]，所以他只好又买了一把新斧子。

过了几天，这个人又去砍柴。就在上山的路上，他看到了自己丢了的斧子。原来[8]上次他下山回家的时候，把斧子掉[9]在路上了，所以在家里找不到呢。

他回到家里，再去观察邻居，但是现在他觉得邻居一点儿也不像偷了斧子的人了。

從前，有一個人以砍柴[2]為生[3]。有一天他上山去砍柴，回家以後，發現斧子不見了。他找啊找啊，在家裡到處找，找了好幾遍，怎麼也找不到。

這個人想，斧子到哪兒去了呢？可是怎麼也想不起來。這時，他看見自己的鄰居從門前走過。不知道為什麼，他覺得鄰居看起來有點慌張[4]，好像跟平常不一樣。他想：對了，一定是鄰居把我的斧子偷走了！

這個人越想越覺得自己的懷疑很對，他就開始悄悄地[5]觀察[6]他的鄰居。越觀察他越覺得是鄰居偷了他的斧子。因為沒有證據[7]，所以他只好又買了一把新斧子。

過了幾天，這個人又去砍柴。就在上山的路上，他看到了自己丟了的斧子。原來[8]上次他下山回家的時候，把斧子掉[9]在路上了，所以在家裡找不到呢。

他回到家裡，再去觀察鄰居，但是現在他覺得鄰居一點兒也不像偷了斧子的人了。

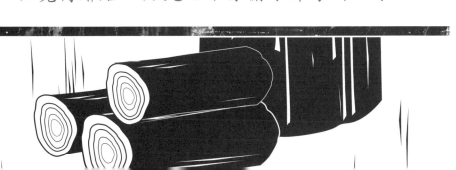

Vocabulary List

	SIMPLIFIED CHARACTERS	TRADITIONAL CHARACTERS	PINYIN	PART OF SPEECH	ENGLISH DEFINITION
1	(怀)疑	(懷)疑	(huái)yí	v./n.	to suspect; doubt
	邻(居)	鄰(居)	lín(jū)	n.	neighbor
	盗	盗	dào	v.	to steal
	斧	斧	fǔ	n.	ax, hatchet
2	砍柴	砍柴	kǎnchái	vo.	to cut wood
3	为生	為生	wéishēng	v.	to make a living
4	慌张	慌張	huāngzhāng	adj.	nervous
5	悄悄地	悄悄地	qiāoqiāo de	adv.	secretly
6	观察	觀察	guānchá	v.	to observe
7	证据	證據	zhèngjù	n.	evidence
8	原来	原來	yuánlái	ce.	it turned out to be
9	掉	掉	diào	v.	to drop, to fall

Questions

1

How does the man in this story make a living?

A. He is an executioner.

B. He is a farmer.

C. He is a woodcutter.

D. He is a bandit.

2

Why does the man suspect his neighbor of stealing his ax?

A. He saw his neighbor bringing lumber back from the woods.

B. He thought his neighbor looked nervous.

C. His neighbor had asked him about the ax earlier.

D. His neighbor had a new wooden gate.

3

What did the man do to find out?

A. He followed his neighbor whenever he went into the woods.

B. He snuck into his neighbor's house late at night.

C. He secretly observed his neighbor.

D. He confronted his neighbor and asked him about it.

4

Because the man had no proof, he

A. bought another ax.

B. planted another ax to see if his neighbor would take it.

C. demanded his neighbor buy him a new ax.

D. stole an ax from his neighbor.

5

What happened to the original ax?

A. The man had left it in the woods.

B. The neighbor found it and gave it back.

C. The man had dropped it in a river.

D. The man had dropped it along the road.

6

After the man found his ax, he

A. felt that his neighbor didn't look like someone who would steal an ax after all.

B. apologized to his neighbor for accusing him of stealing.

C. trusted his neighbor and offered to let him borrow his tools.

D. kept his tools away from his neighbor.

7

Which sentence best describes the moral of this story?

A. Never wrong your neighbors.

B. A suspicious mind may see more than what is really there.

C. Protect the tools that are one's livelihood above all else.

D. Jealousy breeds suspicion.

DISCUSSION

1. Have you ever had a similar experience of wrongly suspecting someone, or being wrongly suspected yourself? Try to retell as much of your story in Chinese as you can.

2. Are there any similar stories about unwarranted suspicion in your own culture? How are they similar to or different from this story?

3

The Man from the State of Qi Who Feared the Sky Would Fall

杞人忧天[1]
杞人憂天[1]

Qǐ rén yōu tiān

中国古代₂，有一个杞国人，他每天都在担心₃会有什么不幸₄的事情要发生₅。这个杞国人最担心的事就是天会塌下来，更糟糕的是他不知道哪一天会塌下来。他觉得天塌下来是最可怕的事情。如果天真的塌下来的话，自己该怎么办呢？要是能躲₆到一个安全₇的地方去就好了，可是他想来想去，想不出一个安全的地方。而且他又不知道是哪一天，就是躲过了今天，也躲不过明天呀！

就这样，这个杞国人越想越担心，越想越害怕₈，不知道怎么办才好。因为太害怕了，所以他吃不好饭，睡不好觉。他的朋友们知道他为什么担心以后，都觉得他又可笑₉，又可怜₁₀。朋友们对他说："你为什么要担心一件不会发生的事呢？天上有太阳、有月亮₁₁，它那么高，那么远，它是不会塌下来的。你每天这样担心、害怕，是一点儿帮助也没有的啊！"杞国人听了朋友的话，还是很担心，很快就因为担心太多，生病死了。

中國古代[2]，有一個杞國人，他每天都在擔心[3]會有什麼不幸[4]的事情要發生[5]。這個杞國人最擔心的事就是天會塌下來，更糟糕的是他不知道哪一天會塌下來。他覺得天塌下來是最可怕的事情。如果天真的塌下來的話，自己該怎麼辦呢？要是能躲[6]到一個安全[7]的地方去就好了，可是他想來想去，想不出一個安全的地方。而且他又不知道是哪一天，就是躲過了今天，也躲不過明天呀！

就這樣，這個杞國人越想越擔心，越想越害怕[8]，不知道怎麼辦才好。因為太害怕了，所以他吃不好飯，睡不好覺。他的朋友們知道他為什麼擔心以後，都覺得他又可笑[9]，又可憐[10]。朋友們對他說："你為什麼要擔心一件不會發生的事呢？天上有太陽、有月亮[11]，它那麼高，那麼遠，它是不會塌下來的。你每天這樣擔心、害怕，是一點兒幫助也沒有的啊！"杞國人聽了朋友的話，還是很擔心，很快就因為擔心太多，生病死了。

Vocabulary List

the man from the state of qi who feared the sky would fall 杞人忧天

	SIMPLIFIED CHARACTERS	TRADITIONAL CHARACTERS	PINYIN	PART OF SPEECH	ENGLISH DEFINITION
1	杞(国)人	杞(國)人	Qǐ(guó)rén	n.	a person from the state of Qi
	忧	憂	yōu	v.	to fear, to worry about
2	古代	古代	gǔdài	n.	ancient times
3	担心	擔心	dānxīn	v.	to fear, to worry
4	不幸	不幸	bùxìng	adj.	unfortunate
5	发生	發生	fāshēng	v.	to happen
6	躲	躲	duǒ	v.	to hide
7	安全	安全	ānquán	adj.	safe
8	害怕	害怕	hàipà	v.	to be afraid of
9	可笑	可笑	kěxiào	adj.	absurd, ridiculous
10	可怜	可憐	kělián	adj.	pitiful
11	月亮	月亮	yuèliang	n.	moon

Questions

1 What made the man so worried about the sky falling?

A. He knew what day the sky would fall.

B. He could not save his family from the falling sky.

C. He would lose all of his wealth and possessions if the sky fell.

D. He did not know what day the sky would fall.

2 Where did the man plan to hide when the sky fell?

A. In a cave.

B. In his house.

C. In a lake.

D. He could not think of a safe place to hide.

3 The man was so worried that he could not even

A. look up at the sky.

B. talk with his friends.

C. eat or sleep.

D. remember where he was.

4 How did the man's friends react when he told them about his fears?

A. They thought he was crazy.

B. They thought his fears were both laughable and pitiful.

C. They thought he should be ignored.

D. They thought he might be right to be worried.

5 What did the man's friends say to try to reassure him?

A. The sun, the moon, and the sky were too far away to fall.

B. The sky was strong enough to support the weight of the sun and the moon.

C. The sun, the moon, and the sky were too large to fall.

D. The sky was holding the sun and the moon in place.

6 How did the man feel after listening to his friends?

A. He was completely relieved.

B. He was a little less worried.

C. He was still worried, but learned to live with his fears.

D. He was still worried, and soon fell ill and died.

7 Which sentence best describes the moral of this story?

A. You should not worry about what you cannot control.

B. There are many worrisome things in the world.

C. Worrying too much can be fatal.

D. The sky cannot fall.

DISCUSSION	2. What do you fear the most? Do you think any of your fears are "groundless"? Try to describe as many of your fears in Chinese as you can.
1. Online, research the state of Qi. When did the state of Qi exist? In roughly what part of modern China was it located?	3. Are there any stories about groundless fears in your own culture? How are they similar to or different from this story?

此地無銀三百兩

此地无银三百兩

4

There Is No Silver Buried Here!

此地无银三百两₁

此地無銀三百兩₁

Cǐ dì wú yín sān bǎi liǎng

此地无银三百两　there is no silver buried here!　SIMPLIFIED

24

中国古时候，在一个集市旁边住着两个人，一个叫<u>张三</u>，一个叫<u>王二</u>。这两个人是邻居，两家的房子中间只有一面₂墙。墙不高，站在这边就能看到那边。

<u>张三</u>在集市上做一点小买卖，他每天很早起床，很晚睡觉，辛辛苦苦地工作。他最大的愿望₃就是赚₄到三百两银子，把它们藏₅起来慢慢地₆花。他想，赚到三百两银子以后，他就可以不用那么辛苦地工作了。

过了很多年，<u>张三</u>终于赚到了三百两银子。他高兴极了，但是也开始担心，不知道应该₇把这些银子放在什么地方。中国古代

中國古時候，在一個集市旁邊住著兩個人，一個叫<u>張三</u>，一個叫<u>王二</u>。這兩個人是鄰居，兩家的房子中間只有一面₂牆。牆不高，站在這邊就能看到那邊。

　　<u>張三</u>在集市上做一點小買賣，他每天很早起床，很晚睡覺，辛辛苦苦地工作。他最大的願望₃就是賺₄到三百兩銀子，把它們藏₅起來慢慢地₆花。他想，賺到三百兩銀子以後，他就可以不用那麼辛苦地工作了。

　　過了很多年，<u>張三</u>終於賺到了三百兩銀子。他高興極了，但是也開始擔心，不知道應該₇把這些銀子放在什麼地方。中國古代沒有銀行，錢只能帶在身上或者藏起來。三百兩銀子帶在身上又重、又不方便，天天帶著也不可能，很容易被別人

没有银行，钱只能带在身上或者藏起来。三百两银子带在身上又重、又不方便，天天带着也不可能，很容易被别人看出来，藏起来最好。可是藏在哪儿呢？藏在外面吧，如果被人发现了、偷走了，怎么办呢？张三想来想去，觉得只有藏在家里最安全，所以他决定₈在家里找一个地方把银子藏起来。

张三在房子里走来走去，走了半天也找不到一个安全的地方，他觉得银子藏在哪儿都不安全，都有可能被人找到，最后他决定在院子₉里挖₁₀一个洞₁₁，把银子埋₁₂在地下。一天晚上，他悄悄地起床，在院子里的一棵大树下面挖了一个洞，把三百两银子埋下去，再小心地把地面踩平，直到一点儿也看不出被挖过的样子。这样做好以后，他正想回去睡觉，可是又一想：不行，如果有人发现了这个洞，把银子挖走了怎么办？他觉得一定得告诉人家，这儿没有银子。所以他回家写了一张纸条，上面写着："此地无银三百两"，意思₁₃是说，"我这儿没有三百两银子。"然后他把纸条贴在大树上。贴好纸条以后，张三才高高兴兴地回去睡觉。

此地无银三百两 SIMPLIFIED

there is no silver buried here!

看出來，藏起來最好。可是藏在哪兒呢？藏在外面吧，如果被人發現了、偷走了，怎麼辦呢？張三想來想去，覺得只有藏在家裡最安全，所以他決定₈在家裡找一個地方把銀子藏起來。

　　張三在房子裡走來走去，走了半天也找不到一個安全的地方，他覺得銀子藏在哪兒都不安全，都有可能被人找到，最後他決定在院子₉裡挖₁₀一個洞₁₁，把銀子埋₁₂在地下。一天晚上，他悄悄地起床，在院子裡的一棵大樹下面挖了一個洞，把三百兩銀子埋下去，再小心地把地面踩平，直到一點兒也看不出被挖過的樣子。這樣做好以後，他正想回去睡覺，可是又一想：不行，如果有人發現了這個洞，把銀子挖走了怎麼辦？他覺得一定得告訴人家，這兒沒有銀子。所以他回家寫了一張紙條，上面寫著："此地無銀三百兩"，意思₁₃是說，"我這兒沒有三百兩銀子。"然後他把紙條貼在大樹上。貼好紙條以後，張三才高高興興地回去睡覺。

此地无银三百两

没想到，张三挖洞的声音[14]被他的邻居王二听到了。他悄悄地来到墙边，正好看到张三在埋银子。第二天早上，王二等到张三出门以后，就爬过墙，来到张三家的院子里，把张三昨天晚上埋的三百两银子都挖了出来。他正想拿了银子回家去，忽然看到大树上的纸条。王二想，那我也得告诉张三我没有偷他的银子，要不然，他一定会怀疑是我偷的。所以王二也回家写了一张纸条，上面写着："隔壁[15]王二不曾[16]偷"，意思是说，"你的邻居王二没有偷你的银子。"王二写好纸条以后，把它贴在张三的纸条旁边，然后就高高兴兴地拿着银子回家去了。

沒想到，張三挖洞的聲音14被他的鄰居王二聽到了。他悄悄地來到牆邊，正好看到張三在埋銀子。第二天早上，王二等到張三出門以後，就爬過牆，來到張三家的院子裡，把張三昨天晚上埋的三百兩銀子都挖了出來。他正想拿了銀子回家去，忽然看到大樹上的紙條。王二想，那我也得告訴張三我沒有偷他的銀子，要不然，他一定會懷疑是我偷的。所以王二也回家寫了一張紙條，上面寫著："隔壁15王二不曾16偷"，意思是說，"你的鄰居王二沒有偷你的銀子。"王二寫好紙條以後，把它貼在張三的紙條旁邊，然後就高高興興地拿著銀子回家去了。

隔壁王二 不曾偷

Vocabulary List

	SIMPLIFIED CHARACTERS	TRADITIONAL CHARACTERS	PINYIN	PART OF SPEECH	ENGLISH DEFINITION
1	此	此	cǐ	pron.	here
	地(方)	地(方)	dì(fang)	n.	place
	无	無	wú	v.	to not have, to be without
	银(子)	銀(子)	yín(zi)	n.	silver, money
	两	兩	liǎng	mw.	(measure word for silver)
2	面	面	miàn	mw.	(measure word for wall)
3	愿望	願望	yuànwàng	n.	wish
4	赚	賺	zhuàn	v.	to earn
5	藏	藏	cáng	v.	to hide
6	慢慢地	慢慢地	mànmàn de	adv.	slowly

	SIMPLIFIED CHARACTERS	TRADITIONAL CHARACTERS	PINYIN	PART OF SPEECH	ENGLISH DEFINITION
7	应该	應該	yīnggāi	av.	should
8	决定	決定	juédìng	v.	to decide
9	院子	院子	yuànzi	n.	yard
10	挖	挖	wā	v.	to dig
11	洞	洞	dòng	n.	hole
12	埋	埋	mái	v.	to bury
13	意思	意思	yìsi	n.	meaning
14	声音	聲音	shēngyīn	n.	sound, noise
15	隔壁	隔壁	gébì	n.	next door
16	不曾	不曾	bùcéng	adv.	did not (do something)

Zhang San wanted to earn three hundred pieces of silver because

A. three hundred is a lucky number.

B. he would no longer have to work so hard.

C. he could then afford to start a business.

D. he would then be richer than his neighbor, Wang Er.

Why did Zhang San need to hide his silver at home?

A. There were no banks in ancient China.

B. The silver was too heavy to carry around with him.

C. People might have been able to find the silver if he hid it away from home.

D. All of the above.

Where did Zhang San hide his silver?

A. Under his bed.

B. Inside the walls of his house.

C. In a hole in his yard.

D. In his neighbor's yard.

4 After hiding his silver, Zhang San left a note in order to

A. avoid arousing suspicion that the silver was hidden in his yard.

B. play a trick on his neighbor.

C. warn against trespassers.

D. encourage people to look after his silver.

5 How did Wang Er know where Zhang San hid the silver?

A. He noticed that Zhang San did not completely cover up the hole.

B. He overheard Zhang San talking to himself in his sleep.

C. He heard and saw Zhang San burying the silver.

D. He read the note that Zhang San had left.

6 After stealing Zhang San's silver, Wang Er left a note saying that

A. there was no silver hidden in his yard.

B. he stole the silver from Zhang San.

C. there was silver hidden in his yard.

D. he did not steal the silver from Zhang San.

7 Which sentence best describes the moral of this story?

A. A fool and his money are soon parted.

B. One must be very careful when hiding something from others.

C. One should never keep secrets.

D. Trying to cover up a secret can unintentionally expose it.

DISCUSSION

1. What do you think happened after Zhang San left his note? Write a short continuation of the story in Chinese.

2. Are you familiar with the story about a man who drew a snake and added feet (画蛇添足/畫蛇添足)? If not, refer to Story 3 of *Tales and Traditions*, Volume 1 or read about the story online. What do you think these two stories have in common?

葉公好龍

叶公好龙

5

Ye Gong Loves Dragons

叶公好龙[1]
葉公好龍[1]

Yè Gōng hào lóng

很

久很久以前，有一个人名字叫"叶公"，也就是叶先生。

叶公有一个最大的爱好，就是非常喜欢龙。在他家里，到处都有龙的图画。他家的房顶$_2$上、墙上画着龙；柱子$_3$上、门上、窗户$_4$上、家具上都雕刻$_5$着龙；他平常穿的衣服、用的东西上都一定要有龙的图案$_6$。叶公不但把自己的家布置$_7$成一个龙的世界$_8$，而且他自己也非常喜欢画龙。他画的龙特别好，看上去就像真的龙一样。他常常对别人说，他最大的愿望就是能看到真的龙。

天上的龙听说叶公这么喜欢它，非常高兴，它也很想满足$_9$叶公的愿望。一天晚上，龙真的来到了叶公的家。它到了叶公家的院子里，在窗子里看到叶公正在睡觉。它想进去看一看叶公，就把头伸进了叶公家的窗户。

久很久以前，有一個人名字叫
"葉公"，也就是葉先生。

　　葉公有一個最大的愛好，就是非常
喜歡龍。在他家裡，到處都有龍的圖畫。他
家的房頂₂上、牆上畫著龍；柱子₃上、門
上、窗戶₄上、家具上都雕刻₅著龍；他平
常穿的衣服、用的東西上都一定要有龍的
圖案₆。葉公不但把自己的家布置₇成一個
龍的世界₈，而且他自己也非常喜歡畫龍。
他畫的龍特別好，看上去就像真的龍一
樣。他常常對別人說，他最大的願望就是
能看到真的龍。

　　天上的龍聽說葉公這麼喜歡它，非常
高興，它也很想滿足₉葉公的願望。一天
晚上，龍真的來到了葉公的家。它到了葉公
家的院子裡，在窗子裡看到葉公正在睡覺。

这时，<u>叶公</u>被龙带来的雷电惊醒[10]了。他张开眼睛，看到一条真的龙就在自己前面，它的身体快把他的家挤破[11]了。<u>叶公</u>吓坏了，就飞快地[12]跑走了。从那以后，<u>叶公</u>再也不说自己喜欢龙了。

人们听说了这件事以后，才知道叶公喜欢的只是画上的龙，而不是真正的龙。他说的和他做的不是一样的。

叶公被龙带来的雷电

惊醒了

葉公再也不說
自己喜歡龍了

它想進去看一看葉公，就把頭伸進了葉公家的窗戶。這時，葉公被龍帶來的雷電驚醒10了。他張開眼睛，看到一條真的龍就在自己前面，它的身體快把他的家擠破11了。葉公嚇壞了，就飛快地12跑走了。從那以後，葉公再也不說自己喜歡龍了。

人們聽說了這件事以後，才知道葉公喜歡的只是畫上的龍，而不是真正的龍。他說的和他做的不是一樣的。

Vocabulary List

	SIMPLIFIED CHARACTERS	TRADITIONAL CHARACTERS	PINYIN	PART OF SPEECH	ENGLISH DEFINITION
1	叶公	葉公	Yè Gōng	pn.	(name of a person)
	好	好	hào	v.	to love, to favor
2	房顶	房頂	fángdǐng	n.	roof
3	柱子	柱子	zhùzi	n.	pillar
4	窗户	窗戶	chuānghu	n.	window
5	雕刻	雕刻	diāokè	v.	to carve
6	图案	圖案	tú'àn	n.	pattern
7	布置	布置	bùzhì	v.	to decorate
8	世界	世界	shìjiè	n.	world
9	满足	滿足	mǎnzú	v.	to satisfy
10	惊醒	驚醒	jīngxǐng	v.	to wake with a start
11	挤破	擠破	jǐpò	vc.	to break
12	飞快地	飛快地	fēikuài de	adv.	swiftly

Questions

1 Which of the following was not in Ye Gong's possession?

  A. Paintings of dragons on his roof and walls.
  B. Carvings of dragons on his pillars, doors, windows, and furniture.
  C. Patterns of dragons on his clothing and everything he used.
  D. Paintings of dragons that could come to life.

2 Ye Gong's greatest wish was to

  A. paint the greatest portrait of a dragon.
  B. fight a real dragon.
  C. see a real dragon.
  D. become a real dragon.

3 Why did the dragon want to visit Ye Gong?

  A. He wanted Ye Gong to paint his portrait.
  B. He wanted to scare Ye Gong.
  C. He wanted to fight Ye Gong.
  D. He wanted Ye Gong's wish to come true.

4 One night, Ye Gong was awakened by

  A. the roar of the dragon.
  B. the heat of the fire from the dragon's breath.
  C. the thunder and lightning brought about by the dragon.
  D. the smell of smoke from the dragon's breath.

5 How did Ye Gong react when he was woken up?

A. He unsheathed his sword and tried to fight off the dragon.

B. He was frightened and quickly ran away.

C. He grabbed a brush and tried to paint the dragon's portrait.

D. He was overwhelmed with joy and fainted.

6 How did Ye Gong change after encountering the dragon?

A. He no longer said that he liked dragons.

B. He became scared whenever he saw an image of a dragon.

C. He got rid of all of his possessions that had to do with dragons.

D. He became even more infatuated with dragons.

7 Which sentence best describes the moral of this story?

A. A love for something can easily turn into hatred.

B. It can be dangerous to boast about one's hobbies.

C. A self-proclaimed love might actually be a façade.

D. You can do anything you put your mind to.

DISCUSSION

1. Does the story about Ye Gong remind you of someone you know? Explain as best you can in Chinese.

2. Using resources online, find out what characteristic(s) are associated with the dragon in Chinese culture. Based on this information, why do you think Ye Gong claimed that he loved dragons so much?

3. What do dragons represent in your culture? In what ways are they similar to or different from Chinese dragons?

6

Yu Gong Removes the Mountains

愚公移山₁
愚公移山₁

Yú Gōng yí shān

中国古时候，有一个小村子。这个小村子在很深很深的山里面，这些大山里有两座最高，把村里人到外面去的路都挡₂住了。

这个村子里住着两个老人，一个非常固执₃，如果他决定了要做一件事，就一定要做到。村里人都叫他"愚公"，意思是"固执的老爷爷"。村里还有另外一个老人，他自己觉得自己非常聪明，对别人做的事常常有不同的看法。他读过很多书，所以村里人都叫他"智叟₄"，意思是"聪明的老爷爷"。

愚公年轻₅的时候，如果要出门去办事，都得爬过两座大山，很不方便。到了他老年的时候，他觉得门前的这两座大山对村里的人来说太不方便了，于是就决定把它们挖走。他把自己家的人都叫来，开始一点一点地挖山。村里的人觉得愚公的想法很对，

中國古時候，有一個小村子。這個小村子在很深很深的山裡面，這些大山裡有兩座最高，把村裡人到外面去的路都擋₂住了。

這個村子裡住著兩個老人，一個非常固執₃，如果他決定了要做一件事，就一定要做到。村裡人都叫他"<u>愚公</u>"，意思是"固執的老爺爺"。村裡還有另外一個老人，他自己覺得自己非常聰明，對別人做的事常常有不同的看法。他讀過很多書，所以村裡人都叫他"<u>智叟</u>₄"，意思是"聰明的老爺爺"。

<u>愚公</u>年輕₅的時候，如果要出門去辦事，都得爬過兩座大山，很不方便。到了他老年的時候，他覺得門前的這兩座大山對村裡的人來說太不方便了，於是就決定

也都一起来参加。就这样，村里就忙起来了，每天都有很多人在山下挖土，挑₆土。

　　智叟看到愚公这么做，觉得很可笑。他对愚公说："你已经这么老了，为什么还要做这样的傻事₇啊？这两座山这么高，你怎么可能把它挖走呢？"愚公笑着回答₈说："真正傻的人不是我，是你呀！你想，我的年纪虽然大了，可是我还有儿子、孙子，孙子又有孙子，子子孙孙一直下去。村里的人也都一样。这两座山虽然很高，但是它再也不会长高了。山上的土，我们挖一点，就会少一点，只要我们一直挖下去，山再高也是可以挖平的啊！"大家都说愚公说得对。

　　最后，天上的玉皇大帝₉听说了愚公挖山的故事，非常感动₁₀，就派₁₁了两个力气₁₂很大的神仙₁₃下来，把两座大山背₁₄走了。从那以后，那两座大山没有了，村子里的人出门再也不用爬山了。

把它們挖走。他把自己家的人都叫來，開始一點一點地挖山。村裡的人覺得愚公的想法很對，也都一起來參加。 就這樣，村裡就忙起來了，每天都有很多人在山下挖土，挑₆土。

　　智叟看到愚公這麼做，覺得很可笑。他對愚公說︰"你已經這麼老了，為什麼還要做這樣的傻事₇啊？這兩座山這麼高，你怎麼可能把它挖走呢？"愚公笑著回答₈說：﹁真正傻的人不是我，是你呀！你想，我的年紀雖然大了，可是我還有兒子、孫子，孫子又有孫子，子子孫孫一直下去。村裡的人也都一樣。這兩座山雖然很高，但是它再也不會長高了。山上的土，我們挖一點，就會少一點，只要我們一直挖下去，山再高也是可以挖平的啊！﹂大家都說愚公說得對。

　　最後，天上的玉皇大帝₉聽說了愚公挖山的故事，非常感動₁₀，就派₁₁了兩個力氣₁₂很大的神仙₁₃下來，把兩座大山背₁₄走了。從那以後，那兩座大山沒有了，村子裡的人出門再也不用爬山了。

Vocabulary List

	SIMPLIFIED CHARACTERS	TRADITIONAL CHARACTERS	PINYIN	PART OF SPEECH	ENGLISH DEFINITION
1	愚公	愚公	Yú Gōng	pn.	(name of a person [lit. Foolish Old Man])
	移	移	yí	v.	to move away
2	挡	擋	dǎng	v.	to block
3	固执	固執	gùzhí	adj.	stubborn
4	智叟	智叟	Zhì Sǒu	pn.	(name of a person [lit. Smart Old Man])
5	年轻	年輕	niánqīng	adj.	young
6	挑	挑	tiāo	v.	to carry on the shoulder
7	傻事	傻事	shǎshì	np.	silly things
8	回答	回答	huídá	v.	to answer
9	玉皇大帝	玉皇大帝	Yùhuáng Dàdì	pn.	the Jade Emperor
10	感动	感動	gǎndòng	v.	to move or be moved, to touch or be touched (emotionally)
11	派	派	pài	v.	to dispatch
12	力气	力氣	lìqi	n.	strength
13	神仙	神仙	shénxiān	n.	immortal, supernatural being
14	背	背	bēi	v.	to carry on the back

Questions

1 The roads leading out of the village were blocked by

    A. deep water.

    B. two tall mountains.

    C. a thick forest.

    D. two long rivers.

2 After scaling these obstacles his whole life, Yu Gong wanted to

    A. climb both peaks one last time.

    B. build a canal to channel water into the village.

    C. remove the mountains completely.

    D. widen the road that passes through the mountains.

3 What did people think of Yu Gong's idea?

    A. The villagers disagreed and Zhi Sou agreed.

    B. The villagers agreed and Zhi Sou disagreed.

    C. Both the villagers and Zhi Sou agreed.

    D. Both the villagers and Zhi Sou disagreed.

4 After hearing about Yu Gong, the Heavenly God

    A. laughed at the old man's foolishness.

    B. opposed the old man's ambitions and became angry.

    C. descended from the heavens to stop the old man.

    D. felt moved by the old man's devotion and decided to help.

5. Which sentence best describes the moral of this story?

A. It is better to be satisfied with the way things are.

B. Pushing through a difficult task can produce surprising results.

C. It is better to leave difficult tasks for future generations.

D. One should not interfere with nature.

DISCUSSION

1. Do you know any stories from another culture that have a similar message?

2. Have you read the story "Bird Jingwei Fills Up the Sea" (精卫填海 / 精衛填海) or "Kua Fu Chases the Sun" (夸父追日)? If not, refer to Story 18 or 22 of *Tales and Traditions*, Volume 1 or research either story online. How is Yu Gong similar to Jingwei or Kua Fu?

3. Explain how these stories encourage or discourage ambitious behavior, and how they depict the relationship between humanity and nature. Does any of this surprise you? Why or why not?

7

Fox Puts on Tiger's Power

狐假虎威₁
狐假虎威₁

Hú jiǎ hǔ wēi

从前，在一座很大的森林$_2$里住着很多动物。森林里有一只老虎，它是这座森林里最强壮$_3$、最有力的动物，所有$_4$的动物都害怕它，一看到老虎来了，就都跑得远远的，或者赶快躲起来。这只老虎非常得意$_5$，它经常在森林里走来走去，到处显示$_6$它的威风$_7$，觉得自己真了不起$_8$。

有一天，老虎正在森林走着，忽然一只狐狸从树丛$_9$里跳了出来，跳到老虎面前。原来这只狐狸没有看到老虎，所以才撞上了它。老虎很生气，它一把捉住这只大胆$_{10}$的狐狸，要把狐狸吃了。

狡猾$_{11}$的狐狸看到自己已经不能从老虎手里逃走$_{12}$了，就想出了一个办法。它对老虎说："你不能吃我！"老虎愣住$_{13}$了，它没想到狐狸会这么说，就问："为什么？"狐狸说："玉皇大帝派我来当这个森林的大王，谁敢吃我？"

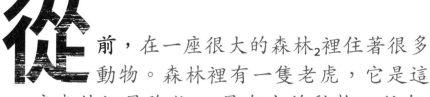

從前，在一座很大的森林2裡住著很多動物。森林裡有一隻老虎，它是這座森林裡最強壯3、最有力的動物，所有4的動物都害怕它，一看到老虎來了，就都跑得遠遠的，或者趕快躲起來。這隻老虎非常得意5，它經常在森林裡走來走去，到處顯示6它的威風7，覺得自己真了不起8。

有一天，老虎正在森林走著，忽然一隻狐狸從樹叢9裡跳了出來，跳到老虎面前。原來這隻狐狸沒有看到老虎，所以才撞上了它。老虎很生氣，它一把捉住這隻大膽10的狐狸，要把狐狸吃了。

狡猾11的狐狸看到自己已經不能從老虎手裡逃走12了，就想出了一個辦法。它對老虎說："你不能吃我！"老虎愣住13了，它沒想到狐狸會這麼說，就問："為什麼？"狐狸說："玉皇大帝派我來當這個

老虎不相信，它说："我从来就是这个森林的大王！"狐狸说："你以前是，现在不是了。现在这个森林里所有的动物都怕我，认为我才是真正的大王。如果你不相信，我们一起在森林里走一走，看看动物们怕不怕我？"

老虎同意了。它让狐狸走在前面，自己跟在后面，看动物们是不是真的怕狐狸。就这样，狐狸抬着头神气₁₄地走在老虎前面，向森林里走去。

动物们看到老虎跟在狐狸的后面，都吓得赶快逃走了。这时，狐狸得意地对老虎说："看到了吗？动物们都怕我呢，因为现在我是森林的大王了！"老虎虽然不同意，但是它也以为动物们现在怕的是狐狸，只好把狐狸放走₁₅了。

森林的大王，誰敢吃我？"老虎
不相信，它說："我從來就是
這個森林的大王！"狐狸說：
"你以前是，現在不是了。現在
這個森林裡所有的動物都怕
我，認為我才是真正的大王。
如果你不相信，我們一起在
森林裡走一走，看看動物們怕
不怕我？"

老虎同意了。它讓狐狸走
在前面，自己跟在後面，看
動物們是不是真的怕狐狸。就
這樣，狐狸抬著頭神氣14地走
在老虎前面，向森林裡走去。

動物們看到老虎跟在狐狸
的後面，都嚇得趕快逃走了。
這時，狐狸得意地對老虎
說："看到了嗎？動物們都怕
我呢，因為現在我是森林的
大王了！"老虎雖然不同意，
但是它也以為動物們現在怕的
是狐狸，只好把狐狸放走15了。

Vocabulary List

	SIMPLIFIED CHARACTERS	TRADITIONAL CHARACTERS	PINYIN	PART OF SPEECH	ENGLISH DEFINITION
1	狐(狸)	狐(狸)	hú(li)	n.	fox
	假	假	jiǎ	v./adj.	to pretend to (be/have); false
	(老)虎	(老)虎	(lǎo)hǔ	n.	tiger
	威(力)	威(力)	wēi(li)	n.	power
2	森林	森林	sēnlín	n.	forest
3	强壮	強壯	qiángzhuàng	adj.	strong
4	所有	所有	suǒyǒu	adj.	all
5	得意	得意	déyì	adj.	complacent, self-satisfied
6	显示	顯示	xiǎnshì	v.	to show, to demonstrate
7	威风	威風	wēifēng	adj.	powerful, imposing
8	了不起	了不起	liǎobùqǐ	adj.	amazing, terrific
9	树丛	樹叢	shùcóng	n.	bushes, thicket
10	大胆	大膽	dàdǎn	adj.	brave
11	狡猾	狡猾	jiǎohuá	adj.	sly, cunning
12	逃走	逃走	táozǒu	vc.	to escape
13	愣住	愣住	lèngzhù	v.	to stun or be stunned
14	神气	神氣	shénqì	adj.	cocky
15	放走	放走	fàngzǒu	vc.	to set free

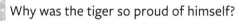

Questions

1 Why was the tiger so proud of himself?

    A. All the animals in the forest loved him.

    B. All the animals in the forest feared him.

    C. He was the smartest animal in the forest.

    D. All the other animals were his servants.

2 How did the fox first encounter the tiger?

    A. The fox taunted the tiger and challenged him to a fight.

    B. The tiger smelled the fox and tracked him down.

    C. The fox did not see the tiger and bumped into him.

    D. The tiger heard the fox and tracked him down.

3 The fox tried to trick the tiger because

    A. he could not escape from the tiger's grip.

    B. he wanted to test the tiger's intelligence.

    C. he could not hunt for food on his own.

    D. he wanted to become the king of the forest.

4 The tiger did not eat the fox because

    A. the fox had an awful smell.

    B. the fox claimed that he was not tasty.

    C. the fox was able to get away.

    D. the fox claimed that he was the new king of the forest.

5 When the fox and the tiger walked through the forest, the other animals

A. smelled the fox and ran away.

B. saw only the fox and ran away.

C. saw the tiger behind the fox and ran away.

D. gathered around to see what was going to happen.

6 Which of the following did the tiger not do after seeing the other animals react?

A. He recognized the fox as the new king of the forest.

B. He thought that the other animals were now afraid of the fox.

C. He disagreed that the fox was the new king of the forest.

D. He decided to let the fox go.

7 Which sentence best describes the moral of this story?

A. It is unwise to speak up against someone stronger than you.

B. Size does not always indicate strength.

C. One can use the strength of another to one's own advantage.

D. It is better to be feared than loved.

DISCUSSION

1. Do you know any stories from another culture that have a similar message?

2. Does the marking on the tiger's forehead in the illustration resemble a Chinese character that you recognize? What qualities do you think the tiger and the fox represent in Chinese culture, and how are the two animals viewed in your own culture?

8

Aiming for the South but Heading for the North

南辕北辙₁
南轅北轍₁

Nán yuán běi zhé

在中国古代，中国分成很多小国。楚国[2]是那时候的一个大国，在中国的南方；魏国[3]也是那时候的一个大国，在中国的北方。

有一天，一个魏国人要到楚国去办事。他挑了一匹跑得最快的马，雇[4]了一个最好的马车夫[5]，带了很多路费[6]，就出发[7]了。可是，他的车不往南方走，却[8]往北方去。

在路上，这个魏国人见到了他的一个好朋友。这个好朋友问他："你这是要上哪儿去啊？"这个魏国人回答说："我要去楚国办点儿事。"

在中國古代，中國分成很多小國。楚國[2]是那時候的一個大國，在中國的南方；魏國[3]也是那時候的一個大國，在中國的北方。

有一天，一個魏國人要到楚國去辦事。他挑了一匹跑得最快的馬，雇[4]了一個最好的馬車夫[5]，帶了很多路費[6]，就出發[7]了。可是，他的車不往南方走，卻[8]往北方去。

在路上，這個魏國人見到了他的一個好朋友。這個好朋友問他："你這是要上哪兒去啊？"這個魏國人回答說："我要去楚國辦點兒事。"

他的朋友覺得很奇怪，就問他："你真的是去楚國嗎？楚國在南邊，但是你現在是往北方走，這不對啊！"

他的朋友觉得很奇怪，就问他："你真的是去楚国吗？楚国在南边，但是你现在是往北方走，这不对啊！"

车不往南方走，
却往北方去

这个魏国人说："没关系，我的马跑得非常快。"他的朋友说："你的马是跑得很快，可这条路不是到楚国去的呀！"

这个魏国人又说："没问题，我的马车夫的技术9非常高，他赶10的马车别人都追不上11。"他的朋友说："你的马车夫技术是很高，可是你让他往北走，他赶的马车走得越快，离楚国也就越远了啊！"

这个魏国人还是满不在乎12地说："没问题，我带了很多路费，一定能到楚国！"他不听朋友的劝告13，一直往北方走去。于是，离他想去的地方越来越远。

這個魏國人說：“沒關系，我的馬跑得非常快。”他的朋友說：“你的馬是跑得很快，可這條路不是到楚國去的呀！”

這個魏國人又說：“沒問題，我的馬車夫的技術[9]非常高，他趕[10]的馬車別人都追不上[11]。”他的朋友說：“你的馬車夫技術是很高，可是你讓他往北走，他趕的馬車走得越快，離楚國也就越遠了啊！”

這個魏國人還是滿不在乎[12]地說：“沒問題，我帶了很多路費，一定能到楚國！”他不聽朋友的勸告[13]，一直往北方走去。於是，離他想去的地方越來越遠。

馬車走得越快，
離楚國也就越遠了

Vocabulary List

	SIMPLIFIED CHARACTERS	TRADITIONAL CHARACTERS	PINYIN	PART OF SPEECH	ENGLISH DEFINITION
1	南	南	nán	n.	south
	辕	轅	yuán	n.	shafts of a wagon
	北	北	běi	n.	north
	辙	轍	zhé	n.	wheel ruts of a wagon
2	楚国	楚國	Chǔguó	pn.	the state of Chu
3	魏国	魏國	Wèiguó	pn.	the state of Wei
4	雇	雇	gù	v.	to hire
5	马车夫	馬車夫	mǎchēfū	n.	cart/wagon driver
6	路费	路費	lùfèi	n.	travel expenses
7	出发	出發	chūfā	v.	to set off, to embark
8	却	卻	què	conj.	but, however
9	技术	技術	jìshù	n.	skill
10	赶	趕	gǎn	v.	to drive
11	追不上	追不上	zhuībùshàng	vc.	to be unable to catch up
12	满不在乎	滿不在乎	mǎnbùzàihu	adj.	giving no heed
13	劝告	勸告	quàngào	n.	advice

Questions

1 Where were the states of Chu and Wei in ancient China?

A. Chu was in the north and Wei was in the south.

B. Chu was in the east and Wei was in the west.

C. Chu was in the south and Wei was in the north.

D. Chu was in the west and Wei was in the east.

2 Who and what did the man from Wei bring with him on his trip?

A. A fast horse, his son, and plenty of food.

B. A fast horse, a skilled horseman, and a map.

C. A fast horse, his son, and plenty of money.

D. A fast horse, a skilled horseman, and plenty of money.

3 Why was the man's friend confused when he heard where the man from Wei was going?

A. The man from Wei had never mentioned the trip to him before.

B. The man from Wei was headed north when he was supposed to be going south.

C. The man from Wei did not bring enough supplies for such a long journey.

D. The man from Wei was headed south when he was supposed to be going north.

4 Which of the following reasons did the man from Wei not give in response to his friend?

A. His horse knew the way to his destination.

B. He had plenty of money for his trip.

C. His horseman was highly skilled.

D. He had the fastest horse in all the land.

5 Which sentence best describes the moral of this story?

A. With sufficient preparation, a destination can always be reached.

B. It is important to place trust in the skills of others.

C. Too much preparation can overcomplicate things.

D. One's actions must be aligned with one's ultimate goal.

DISCUSSION

1. Online, research the states of Chu and Wei. When did these states exist? In roughly what parts of modern China were they located?

2. Do you know the story about how the word for self-contradiction (自相矛盾) came about? If not, refer to Story 6 of *Tales and Traditions*, Volume 1 or read about it online, then compare and contrast the moral of each story.

3. Describe a situation in which it would be appropriate to use the idiom that comes from this story.

伯樂識馬
伯乐识马

9

Bo Le Discovers the Best Horse

伯乐识马₁
伯樂識馬₁

Bó Lè shí mǎ

Bo Le was a famous horse tamer who lived during the Spring and
Autumn period (770–476 B.C.E.). There are many stories about him
that appear in ancient texts such as the *Spring and Autumn Annals*.
Bo Le was renowned for his ability to recognize a good horse, which
was considered an art form in ancient China.

在中国古代，马的作用$_2$非常大。人们骑着它旅行、打仗，也用它来拉车、运输$_3$。但是有的马跑得快，有的马跑得慢，人们都希望得到那种跑得快的好马。那时候有一种好马，它能日行千里，也就是说每天能走一千里，人们把这种马叫作"千里马"。

千里马是最好的马，人人都想得到它，所以能够识别好马、劣$_4$马的人都特别了不起。有一个名字叫伯乐的人，他不管什么样的马，只要看一下，就能够说出它是好马还是劣马，所以大家常常去请他去帮助识别马匹。

有一天，伯乐出门去办事。他在路上看到一匹马正在费力地$_5$拉着一辆车。车上满满的$_6$，很重很重。拉车的马看起来又老又瘦$_7$，它头上流着汗，嘴里流着口水，尾巴$_8$往下垂$_9$着，好像快要走不动了。赶车的人很不耐烦$_{10}$，一直打着它，赶着它，可是它还是走不快。

在中國古代，馬的作用₂非常大。人們騎著它旅行、打仗，也用它來拉車、運輸₃。但是有的馬跑得快，有的馬跑得慢，人們都希望得到那種跑得快的好馬。那時候有一種好馬，它能日行千里，也就是說每天能走一千里，人們把這種馬叫作"千里馬"。

千里馬是最好的馬，人人都想得到它，所以能夠識別好馬、劣₄馬的人都特別了不起。有一個名字叫伯樂的人，他不管什麼樣的馬，只要看一下，就能夠說出它是好馬還是劣馬，所以大家常常去請他去幫助識別馬匹。

有一天，伯樂出門去辦事。他在路上看到一匹馬正在費力地₅拉著一輛車。車上滿滿的₆，很重很重。拉車的馬看起來又老又瘦₇，它頭上流著汗，嘴裡流著口水，尾巴₈往下垂₉著，好像快要走不動了。趕車的人很不耐煩₁₀，一直打著它，趕著它，可是它還是走不快。

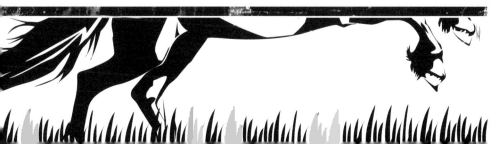

伯乐一眼就看出这是一匹难得的₁₁千里马。他赶快走过去，轻轻地₁₂拍₁₃着马的背，拿出自己的食物给它吃，还脱下₁₄自己的衣服披₁₅在它身上。这匹马好像知道伯乐很喜欢它，它把头靠在₁₆伯乐身上，一直点着头。过了一会儿，它抬起头长长地叫了一声，好像在谢谢伯乐。

赶车的人看到伯乐对这匹马这么喜爱，觉得很奇怪，就问伯乐为什么。伯乐说："你不知道，虽然这匹马现在看起来又老又瘦，可是这是一匹非常难得的千里马呀！你让它来拉车，这太可惜₁₇了，你这是在浪费₁₈它的才能₁₉啊！"伯乐一说完就赶快拿出钱来，把这匹马买下来了。

伯乐把这匹马带回家去，好好照顾₂₀它。过了不久，这匹马长得又高大又强壮，它日行千里，成了有名的千里马。

伯樂一眼就看出這是一匹難得的[11]千里馬。他趕快走過去，輕輕地[12]拍[13]著馬的背，拿出自己的食物給它吃，還脫下[14]自己的衣服披[15]在它身上。這匹馬好像知道伯樂很喜歡它，它把頭靠在[16]伯樂身上，一直點著頭。過了一會兒，它抬起頭長長地叫了一聲，好像在謝謝伯樂。

趕車的人看到伯樂對這匹馬這麼喜愛，覺得很奇怪，就問伯樂為什麼。伯樂說："你不知道，雖然這匹馬現在看起來又老又瘦，可是這是一匹非常難得的千里馬呀！你讓它來拉車，這太可惜[17]了，你這是在浪費[18]它的才能[19]啊！"伯樂一說完就趕快拿出錢來，把這匹馬買下來了。

伯樂把這匹馬帶回家去，好好照顧[20]它。過了不久，這匹馬長得又高大又強壯，它日行千里，成了有名的千里馬。

Vocabulary List

	SIMPLIFIED CHARACTERS	TRADITIONAL CHARACTERS	PINYIN	PART OF SPEECH	ENGLISH DEFINITION
1	识(别)	識(別)	shí(bié)	v.	to distinguish
2	作用	作用	zuòyòng	n.	role
3	运输	運輸	yùnshū	v.	to transport
4	劣	劣	liè	adj.	inferior, bad
5	费力地	費力的	fèilì de	adv.	laboriously
6	满满的	滿滿的	mǎnmǎn de	adj.	full
7	瘦	瘦	shòu	adj.	skinny, thin
8	尾巴	尾巴	wěiba	n.	tail
9	垂	垂	chúi	v.	to hang, to droop
10	不耐烦	不耐煩	bù nàifán	adj.	impatient
11	难得的	難得的	nándé de	adj.	rare, hard to come by
12	轻轻地	輕輕地	qīngqīng de	adv.	gently, lightly
13	拍	拍	pāi	v.	to pat
14	脱下	脫下	tuōxià	vc.	to take off
15	披	披	pī	v.	to drape over the shoulders
16	靠在	靠在	kàozài	v.	to lean on

	SIMPLIFIED CHARACTERS	TRADITIONAL CHARACTERS	PINYIN	PART OF SPEECH	ENGLISH DEFINITION
17	可惜	可惜	kěxī	adj.	pitiful, unfortunate
18	浪费	浪費	làngfèi	adj.	wasteful
19	才能	才能	cáinéng	n.	talent
20	照顾	照顧	zhàogù	v.	to take care of

Questions

1 How long does it take a "one-thousand-*li* horse" to run one thousand *li*?

A. Its entire lifetime.

B. One year.

C. One day.

D. One hour.

2 Bo Le could tell a good horse from a weak one just by

A. riding it for a short distance.

B. measuring its hooves.

C. running alongside it.

D. looking at it.

3 The "one-thousand-*li* horse" that Bo Le saw was

A. young and strong, pulling a cart with strength and vigor.

B. old and thin, sweating and drooling, with its tail hanging downward.

C. young and healthy, but not yet strong enough to pull the cart on its own.

D. old and thin, but pulling the cart slowly and steadily.

4 What did Bo Le give to the horse?

A. Some of his own food and clothes.

B. His own formula to make the horse stronger.

C. An herbal remedy to heal the horse's wounds.

D. Some of his own medicine and clothes.

5 When asked why he treated the horse so well, Bo Le explained that

A. what goes around comes around.

B. the horse would pull the cart faster if cared for properly.

C. having the horse pull a cart was a waste of its abilities.

D. the horse was getting old and needed to retire.

6 What did Bo Le do with the horse?

A. He bought the horse and took good care of it so it would grow tall and strong.

B. He trained the horse before selling it for a high price.

C. He rode the horse for one thousand *li* in search of a new owner.

D. He bought the horse and took good care of it as it grew old and frail.

7 Which kind of person can this story be used to describe?

A. Someone who raises sick animals.

B. A wise old man.

C. Someone who is good at recognizing the abilities of others.

D. A skilled horseman.

DISCUSSION

1. In your culture, how is talent discovered or encouraged?

2. How do you think this story could explain why someone might not be performing a certain task well?

10

Learning to Walk Like the Handan

邯郸学步₁
邯鄲學步₁

Hán dān xué bù

中国古代，有一个城市，叫邯郸。那时人们都觉得邯郸这个地方的人走路的姿势₂特别优美₃。他们走路的时候，又轻快₄、又有风度₅，真是漂亮极了。那时候，很多国家的人都到邯郸来学习走路，去邯郸的路上常常挤满₆了来学习走路的人。很多人来的时候走路的姿势不好看，等到回去的时候，都走得像邯郸人那样姿势优美。

那时候在燕国₇有一个人，他常常觉得燕国人走路的姿势不好看，一点风度都没有。他听说邯郸的人走路的姿势很优美，又看到几个从邯郸回来的人走路的样子真的跟燕国人不一样，姿势特别优美，所以就决定也去邯郸学习。

他旅行了很长的时间才来到邯郸。到了邯郸一看，啊，街上的人走路都那么好看！他赶快找了一个旅店₈住下来。开始的时候，中國古代，有一個城市，叫邯鄲。那時人們都覺得邯鄲這個地方的人走路的姿勢2特別優美3。他們走路的時候，又輕快4、又有風度5，真是漂亮極了。那時候，很多國家的人都到邯鄲來學習走路，去邯鄲的路上常常擠滿6了來學習走路的人。很多人來的時候走路的姿勢不好看，等到回去的時候，都走得像邯鄲人那樣姿勢優美。

那時候在燕國7有一個人，他常常覺得燕國人走路的姿勢不好看，一點風度都沒有。他聽說邯鄲的人走路的姿勢很優美，又看到幾個從邯鄲回來的人走路的樣子真的跟燕國人不一樣，姿勢特別優美，所以就決定也去邯鄲學習。

他每天都站在街道旁边看着街上的人走路，看他们怎么抬头，怎么摆手₉，怎么动脚，怎么迈步₁₀。

邯郸的人走路的姿势很优美

几天以后，这个燕国人也开始模仿₁₁邯郸人的姿势走路了。不过，不管他怎么努力，走起路来就是不像邯郸人。原来他已经有燕国人走路的习惯₁₂了，要学新的姿势很不容易。他只好强迫₁₃自己忘记以前的习惯，一步一步地跟邯郸人学习。

这个燕国人学啊学啊，学了很久，怎么也学不会。他非常失望₁₄。他还想再学下去，但是他的旅费₁₅已经用完了。他只好准备回家。可是，当他想往回走的时候，发现自己已经不知道怎么走路了！他不但没有学会邯郸人走路的姿势，反而₁₆把自己以前走路的习惯也忘了。最后，他只好爬着回到了燕国。

他旅行了很長的時間才來到邯鄲。到了邯鄲一看，啊，街上的人走路都那麼好看！他趕快找了一個旅店[8]住下來。開始的時候，他每天都站在街道旁邊看著街上的人走路，看他們怎麼抬頭，怎麼擺手[9]，怎麼動腳，怎麼邁步[10]。

　　幾天以後，這個燕國人也開始模仿[11]邯鄲人的姿勢走路了。不過，不管他怎麼努力，走起路來就是不像邯鄲人。原來他已經有燕國人走路的習慣[12]了，要學新的姿勢很不容易。他只好強迫[13]自己忘記以前的習慣，一步一步地跟邯鄲人學習。

　　這個燕國人學啊學啊，學了很久，怎麼也學不會。他非常失望[14]。他還想再學下去，但是他的旅費[15]已經用完了。他只好准備回家。可是，當他想往回走的時候，發現自己已經不知道怎麼走路了！他不但沒有學會邯鄲人走路的姿勢，反而[16]把自己以前走路的習慣也忘了。最後，他只好爬著回到了燕國。

最後，他只好
爬著回到了燕國

Vocabulary List

	SIMPLIFIED CHARACTERS	TRADITIONAL CHARACTERS	PINYIN	PART OF SPEECH	ENGLISH DEFINITION
1	步	步	bù	n.	steps (walking style)
2	姿势	姿勢	zīshì	n.	posture
3	优美	優美	yōuměi	adj.	graceful
4	轻快	輕快	qīngkuài	adj.	light and fast
5	风度	風度	fēngdù	adj./n.	stylish, elegant; demeanor
6	挤满	擠滿	jǐmǎn	vc.	to be crowded
7	燕国	燕國	Yānguó	pn.	the state of Yan
8	旅店	旅店	lǚdiàn	n.	hotel, inn
9	摆手	擺手	bǎishǒu	vo.	to move (one's hands)
10	迈步	邁步	màibù	vo.	to step forward
11	模仿	模仿	mófǎng	v.	to imitate
12	习惯	習慣	xíguàn	n.	habit, custom
13	强迫	強迫	qiǎngpò	v.	to force
14	失望	失望	shīwàng	adj.	disappointed
15	旅费	旅費	lǚfèi	n.	travel expenses
16	反而	反而	fǎn'ér	adv.	instead

Questions

The city of Handan was best known for

A. its beautiful scenery.

B. its local delicacies.

C. the way the locals walked.

D. the way the locals talked.

The man from Yan traveled to Handan because he wanted to

A. taste the local cuisine.

B. take in the beautiful scenery.

C. learn the local dialect.

D. learn how to walk like the locals.

After spending days in Handan and not having any luck, the man

A. tried to force himself to forget how to walk.

B. gave up and started to walk home.

C. decided to move to the state of Yan.

D. bought a map to find the scenic spots of the city.

What happened after the man ran out of money and called it quits?

A. He got lost and could not find his way home.

B. He no longer knew how to walk and had to crawl back to the state of Yan.

C. He could not speak the local dialect to ask for directions.

D. He hurt himself and had to crawl back to the state of Yan.

5

Which sentence best describes the moral of this story?

A. Blindly following others can result in losing one's individuality.

B. There is no need to relearn what we already know how to do.

C. We can always improve upon things we already know how to do.

D. It is important to learn how people do things in other societies.

DISCUSSION

1. Why do you think a parent or teacher might tell this story to a child? How do you strike a balance between learning from others and preserving your own individuality?

2. Online, research the state of Yan. When did it exist, and in roughly what part of China was it located? Of which state was Handan the capital, and how far did the man from Yan have to travel?

3. One difference between Chinese and Western cultures is the emphasis on collectivism versus individualism. Using resources online, list some pros and cons of each perspective in a Venn Diagram. Do you relate to one perspective over the other?

II

Tales of Traditional Festivals

第二章　节日传说

第二章　節日傳說

第二章 节日传说

第二章 節日傳說

過年的故事
过年的故事

11

Tales of the Chinese New Year

过年₁的故事
過年₁的故事

Guò nián de gù shi

中国人有自己的历法₂，叫作农历₃。

农历新年的第一天是中国人最重要的节日₄，叫"春节₅"，又叫"新年"。庆祝新年又叫"过年"。过年有很多有意思的庆祝活动。

过年的庆祝活动并不是在农历新年的第一天才开始的，它在农历前一年的十二月中就开始了；过年的庆祝活动也不是在农历新年的第一天就结束₆，它要到一月十五日才结束。

新年的前一天叫"大年三十"。这一天大家都要做年糕₇和很多很多好吃的东西，还要在大门的两旁贴上红色的对联₈，上面写着吉祥₉的话。大年三十的晚上叫作"除夕₁₀"，全家人都坐在一起吃"年夜饭"。年夜饭有鱼有肉，有酒有菜，有饺子有年糕，一家人高高兴兴地一起吃年夜饭，就是要送走过去的一年，迎接₁₁新的一年的到来。

中國人有自己的歷法₂，叫作農曆₃。

農曆新年的第一天是中國人最重要的節日₄，叫"春節₅"，又叫"新年"。慶祝新年又叫"過年"。過年有很多有意思的慶祝活動。

過年的慶祝活動並不是在農曆新年的第一天才開始的，它在農曆前一年的十二月中就開始了；過年的慶祝活動也不是在農曆新年的第一天就結束₆，它要到一月十五日才結束。

新年的前一天叫"大年三十"。這一天大家都要做年糕₇和很多很多好吃的東西，還要在大門的兩旁貼上紅色的對聯₈，上面寫著吉祥₉的話。大年三十的晚上叫作"除夕₁₀"，全家人都坐在一起吃"年夜飯"。年夜飯有魚有肉，有酒有菜，有餃子有年糕，一家人高高興興地一起吃年夜飯，就是要送走過去的一年，迎接₁₁新的一年的到來。

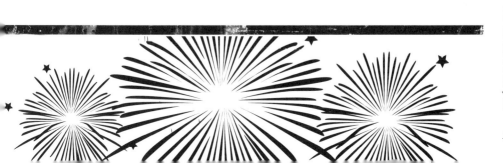

吃完年夜饭，大人小孩都到门口去放鞭炮[12]，然后坐在一起聊天，玩游戏[13]，一夜都不睡觉，叫作"守岁[14]"。因为人们相信，大年三十晚上睡觉的时候如果做了好梦[15]，下一年就会有好运气[16]；如果做了坏梦，下一年的运气就不好。为了不做坏梦，那最好就是不睡觉吧！

新年的第一天叫"大年初一[17]"，大年初一人人都穿上新衣服，互相说着吉祥的话，叫作"拜年[18]"。大人们都给小孩送红包[19]，里面装着压岁钱[20]，希望孩子们在新的一年里平平安安[21]，天天进步。这一天，大家都要吃年糕和汤圆[22]，因为"糕"和"高"发音一样，吃年糕就是希望生活水平一年比一年高的意思；而吃汤圆呢，就是希望一家人团团圆圆[23]，幸福美满[24]地生活在一起，永远不分开。年糕和汤圆都很香很甜[25]，因为人们希望在新的一年里，生活就像年糕和汤圆一样又香又甜。

为什么中国人把庆祝新年叫过年呢？因为这里有一个有趣的故事。古时候，传说有一个妖怪[26]，叫作"年"。年不但长得非常可怕，而且非常凶恶[27]。它平时住在大山里面，但是在农历十二月的最后一天晚上就出来害人[28]，大家都非常害怕它，就把每年的最后一天吃完年夜飯，大人小孩都到門口去放鞭炮[12]，然後坐在一起聊天，玩遊戲[13]，一夜都不睡覺，叫作"守歲[14]"。因為人們相信，大年三十晚上睡覺的時候如果做了好夢[15]，下一年就會有好運氣[16]；如果做了壞夢，下一年的運氣就不好。為了不做壞夢，那最好就是不睡覺吧！

　　新年的第一天叫"大年初一[17]"，大年初一人人都穿上新衣服，互相說著吉祥的話，叫作"拜年[18]"。大人們都給小孩送紅包[19]，裡面裝著壓歲錢[20]，希望孩子們在新的一年裡平平安安[21]，天天進步。這一天，大家都要吃年糕和湯圓[22]，因為"糕"和"高"發音一樣，吃年糕就是希望生活水平一年比一年高的意思；而吃湯圓呢，就是希望一家人團團圓圓[23]，幸福美滿[24]地生活在一起，永遠不分開。年糕和湯圓都很香很甜[25]，因為人們希望在新的一年裡，生活就像年糕和湯圓一樣又香又甜。

　　為什麼中國人把慶祝新年叫過年呢？因為這裡有一個有趣的故事。古時候，傳說有一個妖怪[26]，叫作"年"。年不但長得非常可怕，而且非常凶惡[27]。它平時住在大山裡面，但是在農曆十二月的最後一天晚上就叫作"年关₂₉"，要想过好年关，就要想出好办法来打败凶恶的妖怪年。

团团圆圆
幸福美满

有人说年最害怕的就是红颜色和很大的声音。于是，人们在十二月三十日这天就在大门两边贴上红色的对联，又在门外放鞭炮，这样年就不敢来害人了！它只好回到大山里去了。等到大年初一早上，新的一年开始了，人们很高兴自己平平安安地过了年关，打败了妖怪，所以就把新年叫作过年。因为农历新年也是春季的开始，所以过年也叫"过春节"。

出來害人28，大家都非常害怕它，就把每年的最後一天叫作"年關"29，要想過好年關，就要想出好辦法來打敗凶惡的妖怪年。

有人說年最害怕的就是紅顏色和很大的聲音。於是，人們在十二月三十日這天就在大門兩邊貼上紅色的對聯，又在門外放鞭炮，這樣年就不敢來害人了！它只好回到大山裡去了。等到大年初一早上，新的一年開始了，人們很高興自己平平安安地過了年關，打敗了妖怪，所以就把新年叫作過年。因為農曆新年也是春季的開始，所以過年也叫"過春節"。

Vocabulary List

	SIMPLIFIED CHARACTERS	TRADITIONAL CHARACTERS	PINYIN	PART OF SPEECH	ENGLISH DEFINITION
1	过年	過年	guònián	v.	to celebrate Chinese New Year
2	历法	曆法	lìfǎ	n.	calendar
3	农历	農曆	nónglì	n.	lunar calendar
4	节日	節日	jiérì	n.	holiday
5	春节	春節	Chūnjié	pn.	Spring Festival, Chinese New Year
6	结束	結束	jiéshù	v.	to end
7	年糕	年糕	niángāo	n.	rice cake (for the New Year)
8	对联	對聯	duìlián	n.	antithetical couplet
9	吉祥	吉祥	jíxiáng	adj.	auspicious
10	除夕	除夕	Chúxī	pn.	New Year's Eve
11	迎接	迎接	yíngjiē	v.	to welcome
12	鞭炮	鞭炮	biānpào	n.	firecracker
13	游戏	遊戲	yóuxì	n.	game
14	守岁	守歲	shǒusuì	v.	to keep awake to see the New Year in
15	梦	夢	mèng	n.	dream

	SIMPLIFIED CHARACTERS	TRADITIONAL CHARACTERS	PINYIN	PART OF SPEECH	ENGLISH DEFINITION
16	运气	運氣	yùnqi	n.	luck, fortune
17	大年初一	大年初一	dànián chūyī	n.	New Year's Day
18	拜年	拜年	bàinián	v.	to wish somebody a happy New Year
19	红包	紅包	hóngbāo	n.	red envelope
20	压岁钱	壓歲錢	yāsuìqián	n.	money given for good luck in the New Year
21	平平安安	平平安安	píngpíng 'ān'ān	adj.	peaceful and safe
22	汤圆	湯圓	tāngyuán	n.	sweet dumpling
23	团团圆圆	團團圓圓	tuántuán yuányuán	adj.	(family) reunion
24	美满	美滿	měimǎn	adj.	happy and fulfilled
25	甜	甜	tián	adj.	sweet
26	妖怪	妖怪	yāoguài	n.	monster
27	凶恶	兇惡	xiōng'è	adj.	fierce, ferocious
28	害人	害人	hàirén	vo.	to hurt people
29	年关	年關	niánguān	n.	end of the year

1 The first day of the lunar year is

A. the most important festival in China.

B. called *Chunjie*, or Spring Festival.

C. called *Xinnian*, or New Year's.

D. All of the above.

2 The Chinese New Year festivities last from

A. New Year's Eve to the fifteenth day of the first month.

B. the middle of the twelfth month to the fifteenth day of the first month.

C. New Year's Day to the fifteenth day of the first month.

D. the fifteenth of the twelfth month to New Year's Eve.

3 What do people do the day before New Year's Day?

A. Eat delicious food and write letters to loved ones.

B. Eat delicious food and hang red banners on their doors.

C. Fast while writing letters and preparing food for the next day.

D. Fast while hanging banners and preparing food for the next day.

4 What is not included in the New Year's meal?

A. Fish and meat.

B. Wine and vegetables.

C. Dumplings and *niangao*.

D. Moon cakes and *zongzi*.

5 Why do people not sleep on New Year's Eve?

A. To avoid spirits who haunt people in their sleep.

B. To play games and set off fireworks for as long as possible.

C. To avoid having a bad dream, which would indicate a year of bad luck.

D. Because no one can fall asleep with all the noise from the fireworks.

6 What do children normally find inside a red envelope?

A. Small presents or candies to represent a happy start to the new year.

B. Notes from family members containing well-wishes for the new year.

C. Money for good luck in the new year.

D. Firecrackers to be set off by the front entrance of the home.

7 What do people do to scare off the monster known as Nian?

A. Hang red banners and leave fireworks outside their homes.

B. Hang gold banners and leave fireworks outside their homes.

C. Hang red banners and set off fireworks outside their homes.

D. Hang gold banners and set off fireworks outside their homes.

DISCUSSION

1. Why do people eat 年糕 and 汤圆 / 湯圓 on Chinese New Year? Using resources online, find out why Chinese people eat fish during New Year's. Why do you think people do not eat the entire fish?

2. Research other Chinese New Year traditions online. How is the Spring Festival similar to or different from the traditions observed during New Year's (or other important holidays or festivals) in your culture?

元宵節的傳說

元宵节的传说

12

Tales of the Lantern Festival

元宵节₁的传说
元宵節₁的傳說

Yuán xiāo jié de chuán shuō

农历新年的庆祝活动要到新年的一月十五日才结束。中国农历是按照月亮的圆缺$_2$来设置$_3$的，每个月的第一天和最后一天月亮最缺，第十五天月亮最圆。农历一月十五是过完新年后的第一个圆月，叫"元宵节"。"元"有"第一"和"开始"的意思，"宵"就是晚上的意思。元宵节在中国也是一个重要的节日，它的庆祝活动主要是在晚上。

关于$_4$元宵节也有很多有意思的传说。有一个传说是，古时候天上住着<u>天帝</u>$_5$，他有很多神鸟$_6$。有一天，一只神鸟迷路$_7$了，飞到了人间$_8$。有一个猎人不知道这是一只神鸟，不小心$_9$把它射$_{10}$死了。<u>天帝</u>非常生气，就要天兵天将在新年后的第一个圆月夜把人们都烧死$_{11}$。<u>天帝</u>的女儿知道了这个消息$_{12}$，很难过。为了帮助人们，她悄悄地把这个消息告诉人们，让大家做好准备$_{13}$。开始的时候農歷新年的慶祝活動要到新年的一月十五日才結束。中國農歷是按照月亮的圓缺[2]來設置[3]的，每個月的第一天和最後一天月亮最缺，第十五天月亮最圓。農歷一月十五是過完新年後的第一個圓月，叫"元宵節"。"元"有"第一"和"開始"的意思，"宵"就是晚上的意思。元宵節在中國也是一個重要的節日，它的慶祝活動主要是在晚上。

關於[4]元宵節也有很多有意思的傳說。有一個傳說是，古時候天上住著天帝[5]，他有很多神鳥[6]。有一天，一隻神鳥迷路[7]了，飛到了人間[8]。有一個獵人不知道這是一隻神鳥，不小心[9]把它射[10]死了。天帝非常生氣，就要天兵天將在新年後的第一個圓月夜把人們都燒死[11]。天帝的女兒知道了這個消息[12]，很難過。為了幫助人們，她悄悄地把這個消息告訴人們，讓大家做好准備[13]。開始的時候人們都非常害怕，

放起鞭炮

人们都非常害怕，不知道应该怎么办才好。后来大家想出了一个办法，就是在元月十五这一天晚上，每人都在自己家门口挂起大红灯笼[14]，点上蜡烛[15]，并且放起鞭炮和烟花[16]。这样天帝从天上远远的看下来，只见地上红光一片，以为[17]天兵天将已经把人们都烧死了，就不会再生气了。大家都觉得这个办法很好。

到了元月十五这天晚上，到处都挂起了灯笼，放起了鞭炮、烟花。人们一边看灯笼，一边吃着又香又甜的汤圆，庆祝自己又战胜[18]了一场灾难[19]。后来，为了纪念[20]这次成功[21]，人们就把这一天定为元宵节，年年庆祝，成为中国人最喜欢的节日之一[22]。

不知道應該怎麼辦才好。後來大家想出了一個辦法，就是在元月十五這一天晚上，每人都在自己家門口掛起大紅燈籠[14]，點上蠟燭[15]，並且放起鞭炮和煙花[16]。這樣<u>天帝</u>從天上遠遠的看下來，只見地上紅光一片，以為[17]天兵天將已經把人們都燒死了，就不會再生氣了。大家都覺得這個辦法很好。

到了元月十五這天晚上，到處都掛起了燈籠，放起了鞭炮、煙花。人們一邊看燈籠，一邊吃著又香又甜的湯圓，慶祝自己又戰勝[18]了一場災難[19]。後來，為了紀念[20]這次成功[21]，人們就把這一天定為元宵節，年年慶祝，成為中國人最喜歡的節日之一[22]。

掛起燈籠

Vocabulary List

	SIMPLIFIED CHARACTERS	TRADITIONAL CHARACTERS	PINYIN	PART OF SPEECH	ENGLISH DEFINITION
1	元宵节	元宵節	Yuánxiāojié	pn.	the Lantern Festival
2	缺	缺	quē	adj.	fragmented
3	设置	設置	shèzhì	v.	to design, to arrange
4	关于	關於	guānyú	prep.	about, concerning
5	天帝	天帝	Tiāndì	pn.	Heavenly God
6	神鸟	神鳥	shénniǎo	n.	celestial bird, phoenix
7	迷路	迷路	mílù	vo.	to get lost
8	人间	人間	rénjiān	n.	the human world
9	不小心	不小心	bù xiǎoxīn	adv.	inadvertently
10	射	射	shè	v.	to shoot down
11	烧死	燒死	shāosǐ	vc.	to burn to death
12	消息	消息	xiāoxi	n.	news
13	准备	準備	zhǔnbèi	n.	preparation
14	灯笼	燈籠	dēnglong	n.	lantern
15	蜡烛	蠟燭	làzhú	n.	candle
16	烟花	煙花	yānhuā	n.	fireworks

	SIMPLIFIED CHARACTERS	TRADITIONAL CHARACTERS	PINYIN	PART OF SPEECH	ENGLISH DEFINITION
17	以为	以為	yǐwéi	v.	to believe (incorrectly)
18	战胜	戰勝	zhànshèng	vc.	to triumph over
19	灾难	災難	zāinàn	n.	disaster
20	纪念	紀念	jìniàn	v.	to commemorate
21	成功	成功	chénggōng	n.	success
22	之一	之一	zhīyī	n.	one of

Questions

1 When do most of the festivities for the Lantern Festival take place?

A. The morning of the last day of Chinese New Year.
B. The beginning of Chinese New Year.
C. The evening of the last day of Chinese New Year.
D. The middle of Chinese New Year.

2 According to legend, the Heavenly God was angered when

A. a hunter accidentally shot down a celestial bird.
B. a hunter shot down a celestial bird for a New Year's feast.
C. a celestial bird descended to earth and lived with people.
D. a celestial bird descended to earth and attacked people.

3 What did the Heavenly God plan to do as punishment?

A. Capture the celestial bird and cook it for a heavenly feast.

B. Send the celestial bird to attack the humans.

C. Set the entire earth and its inhabitants on fire.

D. Feed a group of humans to the celestial bird.

4 After receiving a warning from the Heavenly Daughter, how did people prepare?

A. They sealed their doors and blew out all their candles and lanterns.

B. They assembled all of their horses and cannons.

C. They hung red banners on their front doors and hid.

D. They hung red lanterns, lit candles, and set off fireworks.

5 People admire lanterns and eat sweet dumplings to celebrate

A. the celestial bird.

B. overcoming a disaster.

C. the Heavenly God.

D. the beginning of Chinese New Year.

DISCUSSION

1. How are the festivities of 元宵节 / 元宵節 similar to or different from other Chinese New Year traditions?

2. Are there holidays or festivals in your culture that involve making or lighting lanterns? Do you think the significance of lanterns is similar across cultures?

13

The Dragon Boat Festival and the Poet Qu Yuan

端午节₁和屈原
端午節₁和屈原

Duān wǔ jié hé Qū Yuán

Qu Yuan (ca. 340–278 B.C.E.) was a patriotic poet and high-ranking official from the state of Chu who lived during the Warring States period. Despite living in exile for many years, Qu Yuan expressed his love and concern for his state through some of the most influential poems in Chinese literature. His tragic death is commemorated every year during the Dragon Boat Festival.

中国人的第三个有名的传统节日，叫"端午节"。端午节是在农历的五月五日。"端"有开始的意思。农历的每个月都有三天有"五"这个数字，它们是初五、十五、二十五。初五也叫"端五"，因为它是第一个带"五"的日子。五月在古代也叫"午月"。因为五月初五是午月的端五，所以叫端午节。而这一天又是楚国有名的爱国$_2$诗人$_3$屈原投江$_4$自杀的日子。为了纪念屈原，人们在这一天进行$_5$了很多庆祝活动。于是，这个节日就越来越有名了。

中国人每年过端午节的时候，都会想起屈原。屈原是一个有名的诗人，也是楚国的大官。中国在古代分成$_6$好几个小国，有的大一点，有的小一点，但是这些国家互相不友好，常常打仗。楚国和秦国$_7$都是那时候的大国。屈原看到秦国一直在准备打楚国，他

中國人的第三個有名的傳統節日，叫
"端午節"。端午節是在農曆的五月
五日。"端"有開始的意思。農曆的每個月
都有三天有"五"這個數字，它們是初五、
十五、二十五。初五也叫"端五"，因為它
是第一個帶"五"的日子。五月在古代也叫
"午月"。因為五月初五是午月的端五，所以
叫端午節。而這一天又是楚國有名的
愛國2詩人3屈原投江4自殺的日子。為了
紀念屈原，人們在這一天進行5了很多慶祝
活動。於是，這個節日就越來越有名了。

　　中國人每年過端午節的時候，都會想
起屈原。屈原是一個有名的詩人，也是
楚國的大官。中國在古代分成6好幾個小
國，有的大一點，有的小一點，但是這些
國家互相不友好，常常打仗。楚國和秦國7
都是那時候的大國。屈原看到秦國一直在
准備打楚國，他想如果楚國不強大，就會

想如果楚国不强大，就会被秦国打败。为了楚国能够强大，屈原给楚国的国王提了很多很好的建议，希望他能够听他的意见[8]，让楚国强大。可是楚王不听屈原的建议，他不但不听，还听坏人的话，把屈原流放[9]到离楚国很远的地方去。屈原心里非常痛苦[10]，在流放的路上，他写了很多感动人的诗歌，表达[11]了自己对楚国人民的热爱[12]和对楚国命运[13]的担心，为楚王不接受自己的建议而难过。

因为楚王不听屈原的建议，楚国变得越来越糟糕。有一年的五月初五，屈原走到了汨罗江[14]边。过了汨罗江，就不是楚国了。也就在这一天，屈原听到楚国被秦国打败了，楚王也被秦国抓走[15]了。屈原感到非常痛苦，他宁死[16]也不愿意离开自己的国家，于是就跳进汨罗江，自杀了。

楚国的人听说屈原自杀的消息，都非常难过。他们来到汨罗江边，划着[17]小船，在江上来来回回地找，想把屈原找回来。他们还把米饭包在竹叶[18]里，做成粽子[19]，丢[20]到江里去让鱼吃，希望它们不要去伤害[21]屈原。从此，人们每年在五月初五这一天都要在江上举行划船（也叫划龙船）的比赛，还在这一天吃粽子来纪念这位伟大的[22]爱国诗人。

被秦國打敗。為了楚國能夠強大，屈原給楚國的國王提了很多很好的建議，希望他能夠聽他的意見8，讓楚國強大。可是楚王不聽屈原的建議，他不但不聽，還聽壞人的話，把屈原流放9到離楚國很遠的地方去。屈原心裡非常痛苦10，在流放的路上，他寫了很多感動人的詩歌，表達11了自己對楚國人民的熱愛12和對楚國命運13的擔心，為楚王不接受自己的建議而難過。

因為楚王不聽屈原的建議，楚國變得越來越糟糕。有一年的五月初五，屈原走到了汨羅江14邊。過了汨羅江，就不是楚國了。也就在這一天，屈原聽到楚國被秦國打敗了，楚王也被秦國抓走15了。屈原感到非常痛苦，他寧死16也不願意離開自己的國家，於是就跳進汨羅江，自殺了。

楚國的人聽說屈原自殺的消息，都非常難過。他們來到汨羅江邊，划著17小船，在江上來來回回地找，想把屈原找回來。他們還把米飯包在竹葉18裡，做成粽子19，丟20到江裡去讓魚吃，希望它們不要去傷害21屈原。從此，人們每年在五月初五這一天都要在江上舉行划船（也叫划龍船）的比賽，還在這一天吃粽子來紀念這位偉大的22愛國詩人。

Vocabulary List

	SIMPLIFIED CHARACTERS	TRADITIONAL CHARACTERS	PINYIN	PART OF SPEECH	ENGLISH DEFINITION
1	端午节	端午節	Duānwǔjié	pn.	the Dragon Boat Festival
2	爱国(的)	愛國(的)	àiguó (de)	adj.	patriotic
3	诗人	詩人	shīrén	n.	poet
4	投江	投江	tóujiāng	vo.	to jump into a river
5	进行	進行	jìnxíng	v.	to carry out
6	分成	分成	fēnchéng	vc.	to be divided into
7	秦国	秦國	Qínguó	pn.	the state of Qin
8	意见	意見	yìjiàn	n.	idea, opinion
9	流放	流放	liúfàng	v.	to exile
10	痛苦	痛苦	tòngkǔ	adj.	painful, sad
11	表达	表達	biǎodá	v.	to express

	SIMPLIFIED CHARACTERS	TRADITIONAL CHARACTERS	PINYIN	PART OF SPEECH	ENGLISH DEFINITION
12	热爱	熱愛	rè'ài	v.	to love passionately
13	命运	命運	mìngyùn	n.	destiny
14	汨罗江	汨羅江	Mìluójiāng	pn.	(name of a river)
15	抓走	抓走	zhuāzǒu	vc.	to arrest
16	宁死	寧死	nìngsǐ	v.	to rather die
17	划	划	huá	v.	to row (a boat)
18	竹叶	竹葉	zhúyè	n.	bamboo leaves
19	粽子	粽子	zòngzi	n.	sticky rice wrapped in bamboo leaves
20	丢	丢	diū	v.	to drop
21	伤害	傷害	shānghài	v.	to harm
22	伟大的	偉大的	wěidà de	adj.	great

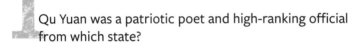

Questions

1 Qu Yuan was a patriotic poet and high-ranking official from which state?

A. Qin

B. Wei

C. Zhao

D. Chu

2 The Dragon Boat Festival falls on the day that Qu Yuan

A. was born.

B. passed away.

C. was exiled.

D. became a high-ranking official.

3 When Qu Yuan made suggestions to the king on how to strengthen the state, the king

A. accused him of treason and sentenced him to solitary confinement.

B. praised him and appointed him as second-in-command.

C. refused to listen and sent him into exile.

D. gave his suggestions some serious consideration.

4 After meeting with the king, Qu Yuan wrote

A. uplifting poems that led the state to victory.
B. moving poems expressing his love for his homeland and concern for its destiny.
C. a powerful manifesto calling for a revolution.
D. a convincing plea begging for the enemy to have mercy on his homeland.

5 What did Qu Yuan do when he received word of the king's capture?

A. He crossed the Miluo River to escape from the state of Chu.
B. He returned to his homeland immediately and offered his help.
C. He jumped in the Miluo River and took his own life.
D. He led a rescue attempt.

6 What did the people of Chu do when they received word of Qu Yuan's whereabouts?

A. They jumped into the river in search of him.
B. They searched for him by boat and put *zongzi* in the river.
C. They went fishing and prepared *zongzi* for a large feast in his honor.
D. They had a race to see who could find him first.

7 How do people celebrate the Dragon Boat Festival today?

A. They hold dragon boat races and eat *zongzi*.

B. They continue to search for Qu Yuan by boat and put *zongzi* in the river.

C. They hold dragon boat races and eat *niangao*.

D. They jump into the water in search of Qu Yuan and put *zongzi* in the river.

DISCUSSION

1. Are there historical figures in your country who are highly revered like Qu Yuan? How are they similar to or different from Qu Yuan?

2. Using resources online, research Qu Yuan's most famous poem. Why do you think this poem is considered to be his most important piece? How is it similar to the story behind the Dragon Boat Festival?

中秋節的故事

中秋节的故事

14

Tales of the Mid-Autumn Festival

中秋节的故事
中秋節的故事

Zhōng qiū jié de gù shi

中秋节也是重要的中国传统节日之一。

农历的七月、八月、九月是秋天，八月是这三个月中间的那一个月，八月十五又是八月中间的那一天，所以中国人把八月十五叫作中秋节，意思是秋天中间的节日。农历每个月的十五那天月亮都是最圆的，而八月十五的月亮是最圆、最亮的。秋天又是收获$_1$的时候，所以在农历八月十五这天晚上，一家人高高兴兴地坐在一起，对着又圆又亮的月亮，吃着又香又甜、看起来像月亮一样的月饼$_2$和瓜果$_3$，快乐地庆祝中秋节。

中秋节的传说也非常有意思。听说很久很久以前，天上有十个太阳。它们把江河里的水都烤干$_4$了，农作物$_5$都旱$_6$死了，人们也又热又渴$_7$，很快都要死了。这时候有一个英雄，他的名字叫<u>后羿$_8$</u>，他一下子就射下了九个太阳，只留下一个。从此，人们过上了

中秋节的故事　SIMPLIFIED　tales of the mid-autumn festival

中秋節也是重要的中國傳統節日之一。農曆的七月、八月、九月是秋天，八月是這三個月中間的那一個月，八月十五又是八月中間的那一天，所以中國人把八月十五叫作中秋節，意思是秋天中間的節日。農曆每個月的十五那天月亮都是最圓的，而八月十五的月亮是最圓、最亮的。秋天又是收穫₁的時候，所以在農曆八月十五這天晚上，一家人高高興興地坐在一起，對著又圓又亮的月亮，吃著又香又甜、看起來像月亮一樣的月餅₂和瓜果₃，快樂地慶祝中秋節。

中秋節的傳說也非常有意思。聽說很久很久以前，天上有十個太陽。它們把江河裡的水都烤乾₄了，農作物₅都旱₆死了，人們也又熱又渴₇，很快都要死了。這時候有一個英雄，他的名字叫后羿₈，他一下子就射下了九個太陽，只留下一個。從此，人們過上了

正常的$_9$生活。因为后羿帮助人们躲过了灾难，大家都非常感激他。

　　后羿的妻子名字叫嫦娥$_{10}$，她长得很漂亮，后羿非常爱她。为了能和嫦娥永远幸福地生活在一起，后羿向天上的王母娘娘$_{11}$要来一些仙药$_{12}$。这些仙药如果一个人吃下去，就能飞到天上去，成为神仙；如果一个人只吃一半，就能永远不死。后羿想和嫦娥两人分吃这些仙药，这样两人可以永远不死，永远在一起。

　　后羿带着仙药回到家里的时候，嫦娥正好不在家。后羿就把药放在桌上，出去找嫦娥，要把这件事告诉她。过了一会儿，嫦娥回来了。她看见桌上的仙药非常可爱，没有等后羿回来，就一下把它们都吃下去了。她刚吃下仙药，就觉得身体轻飘飘的$_{13}$，双脚很快就离开$_{14}$地面了。她什么也没带，只抱走了家里的一只白兔。后羿在家门口看到嫦娥往天上飞去，想去拉她，可是已经太晚了。嫦娥越飞越高，越飞越快，不一会儿，她就飞到高高的月亮上去了。就这样，一对恩爱的$_{15}$夫妻从那天以后就分开了。他们只能一个住在天上，一个住在地上，永远不能在一起了。月亮上虽然有美丽的月宫$_{16}$，但是没有了幸福的家。后羿和嫦娥都非常难过，但是他们一点儿办法也没有。

正常的₉生活。因為后羿幫助人們躲過了災難，大家都非常感激他。

　　后羿的妻子名字叫嫦娥₁₀，她長得很漂亮，后羿非常愛她。為了能和嫦娥永遠幸福地生活在一起，后羿向天上的王母娘娘₁₁要來一些仙藥₁₂。這些仙藥如果一個人吃下去，就能飛到天上去，成為神仙；如果一個人只吃一半，就能永遠不死。后羿想和嫦娥兩人分吃這些仙藥，這樣兩人可以永遠不死，永遠在一起。

　　后羿帶著仙藥回到家裡的時候，嫦娥正好不在家。后羿就把藥放在桌上，出去找嫦娥，要把這件事告訴她。過了一會兒，嫦娥回來了。她看見桌上的仙藥非常可愛，沒有等后羿回來，就一下把它們都吃下去了。她剛吃下仙藥，就覺得身體輕飄飄的₁₃，雙腳很快就離開₁₄地面了。她什麼也沒帶，只抱走了家裡的一隻白兔。后羿在家門口看到嫦娥往天上飛去，想去拉她，可是已經太晚了。嫦娥越飛越高，越飛越快，不一會兒，她就飛到高高的月亮上去了。就這樣，一對恩愛的₁₅夫妻從那天以後就分開了。他們只能一個住在天上，一個住在地上，永遠不能在一起了。月亮上后来，人们因为同情[17]后羿和嫦娥，同时也希望家人都能幸福地生活在一起，永远不分开，就把八月十五这一天定为[18]中秋节。在这一天里，人们对着月亮，庆祝丰收和团圆的喜悦[19]。那些不能回家和家人团圆的人，也常常对着月亮，想念[20]着家里人。传说嫦娥在这一天也在月亮上唱歌跳舞，把明亮的月光洒下来[21]，让人们永远珍惜[22]家人团圆的幸福。就这样，中秋节在中国成了一个庆祝丰收[23]的节日，也是一个庆祝家庭团圆的节日。

庆祝丰收和团圆的喜悦

永遠珍惜家人
團圓的幸福

雖然有美麗的月宮[16]，但是沒有了幸福的家。后羿和嫦娥都非常難過，但是他們一點兒辦法也沒有。

後來，人們因為同情[17]后羿和嫦娥，同時也希望家人都能幸福地生活在一起，永遠不分開，就把八月十五這一天定為[18]中秋節。在這一天裡，人們對著月亮，慶祝豐收和團圓的喜悅[19]。那些不能回家和家人團圓的人，也常常對著月亮，想念[20]著家裡人。傳說嫦娥在這一天也在月亮上唱歌跳舞，把明亮的月光灑下來[21]，讓人們永遠珍惜[22]家人團圓的幸福。就這樣，中秋節在中國成了一個慶祝豐收[23]的節日，也是一個慶祝家庭團圓的節日。

Vocabulary List

	SIMPLIFIED CHARACTERS	TRADITIONAL CHARACTERS	PINYIN	PART OF SPEECH	ENGLISH DEFINITION
1	收获	收穫	shōuhuò	v.	to harvest
2	月饼	月餅	yuèbǐng	n.	moon cake
3	瓜果	瓜果	guāguǒ	n.	vegetables and fruits
4	烤干	烤乾	kǎogān	vc.	to roast dry
5	农作物	農作物	nóngzuòwù	n.	crops
6	旱	旱	hàn	n.	drought
7	渴	渴	kě	adj.	thirsty
8	后羿	后羿	Hòu Yì	pn.	(name of a person)
9	正常的	正常的	zhèngcháng de	adj.	normal
10	嫦娥	嫦娥	Cháng É	pn.	(name of a person)
11	王母娘娘	王母娘娘	Wángmǔ Niángniang	pn.	the Heavenly Queen
12	仙药	仙藥	xiānyào	n.	celestial elixir
13	轻飘飘的	輕飄飄的	qīng piāopiāo de	adj.	buoyant
14	离开	離開	líkāi	vc.	to depart from
15	恩爱的	恩愛的	ēn'ài de	adj.	beloved
16	月宫	月宮	yuègōng	n.	Moon Palace

	SIMPLIFIED CHARACTERS	TRADITIONAL CHARACTERS	PINYIN	PART OF SPEECH	ENGLISH DEFINITION
17	同情	同情	tóngqíng	v.	to sympathize
18	定为	定為	dìngwéi	vc.	to be decided as
19	喜悦	喜悦	xǐyuè	n.	happiness
20	想念	想念	xiǎngniàn	v.	to miss
21	洒下来	灑下來	sǎ xiàlai	vc.	to pour down (as light, water, etc.)
22	珍惜	珍惜	zhēnxī	v.	to cherish
23	丰收	豐收	fēngshōu	n.	abundant harvest

Questions

1 The Mid-Autumn Festival is celebrated during a

A. waxing moon.

B. waning moon.

C. new moon.

D. full moon.

2 What did Houyi do to save people from disaster?

A. He tamed the ten burning suns to nourish the crops.

B. He turned half of the suns into moons.

C. He shot down nine of the suns and left only one in the sky.

D. He shot down all of the suns and left only the moon in the sky.

3 What happened when Houyi brought home the celestial elixir that would allow him and Chang E to be together forever?

A. They each took half and gained immortality.
B. Chang E accidentally took it all and floated up to the moon.
C. Hou Yi accidentally took it all and floated up to the moon.
D. Neither of them took any because they wanted to stay on earth together.

4 When the elixir was all gone, what did Chang E bring with her?

A. The empty bottle.
B. Houyi's bow and arrow.
C. A white rabbit.
D. A mooncake.

5 What do people not do on the evening of the Mid-Autumn Festival?

A. Eat *zongzi* and gaze up at the moon.
B. Eat mooncakes and gaze up at the moon.
C. Reunite with their families.
D. Long for their families.

DISCUSSION

1. How is the shape of the moon reflected in the traditions of the Mid-Autumn Festival? What do you think this shape symbolizes in Chinese culture?

2. Can you see any similarities between the traditions of the Mid-Autumn Festival and Thanksgiving or another holiday in your culture?

3. Online, listen to the song 《但愿人长久》 / 《但願人長久》 from the poem called 《水调歌头》 / 《水調歌頭》 by Su Shi (苏轼 / 蘇軾). What words or phrases can you recognize, and how do they relate to the Mid-Autumn Festival?

III

Myths and Fantasies

第三章　神话故事

第三章　神話故事

15

Cang Jie Invents the Chinese Writing Script

仓颉造字[1]
倉頡造字[1]

Cāng Jié zào zì

While considered a legendary figure, Cang Jie is credited by historical texts such as the *Spring and Autumn Annals* for inventing Chinese characters. He is believed to be the official historian of the Yellow Emperor, who is said to have reigned from 2697 B.C.E. to 2598 B.C.E.

字是美丽的文字，你知道汉字是怎么发明$_2$的吗？

很久很久以前，中国人没有文字，只能用绳子打结$_3$来记录$_4$事情。这种方法很不方便，能记录的东西又很少。你想，要是一个人有100条鱼$_5$，他就得在绳子上打100个结，那多麻烦呀。

一个名字叫仓颉的聪明人下决心$_6$要发明一种更好的方法。他每天想啊想啊，但是想不出来。

有一天，他在地上看到一个奇怪的脚印$_7$，他不认识，就去问一位老猎人$_8$。老猎人看了看，说："这是鸡$_9$的脚印，你看，那脚印又细$_{10}$又长，只有鸡的脚才长成这样。"

仓颉一听这话，高兴极了，不是因为他认识了鸡的脚印，而是他突然$_{11}$想到，世界上的

**漢**字是美麗的文字，你知道漢字是怎麼發明₂的嗎？

很久很久以前，中國人沒有文字，只能用繩子打結₃來記錄₄事情。這種方法很不方便，能記錄的東西又很少。你想，要是一個人有100條魚₅，他就得在繩子上打100個結，那多麻煩呀。

一個名字叫倉頡的聰明人下決心₆要發明一種更好的方法。他每天想啊想啊，但是想不出來。

有一天，他在地上看到一個奇怪的腳印₇，他不認識，就去問一位老獵人₈。老獵人看了看，說："這是雞₉的腳印，你看，那腳印又細₁₀又長，只有雞的腳才長成這樣。"

倉頡一聽這話，高興極了，不是因為他認識了雞的腳印，而是他突然₁₁想到，世界上的東西都有自己的特徵₁₂，只要把

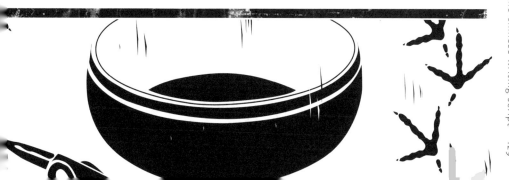

东西都有自己的特征[12]，只
要把这些特征记下来，不就
能代表[13]不同的东西了吗？

然后，仓颉开始认真地
观察起周围[14]的东西来，他
发现[15]太阳是圆圆的，就用
一个圆O来代表太阳；月亮是
弯弯的，那就画一个弯（〗）
吧，山是⌐，小河是≈。就
这样，仓颉画出了越来越多
的图形[16]，他还发现把这些
图形组合[17]在一起，还可以
表达更多的意思。

仓颉把这些图形拿去给
黄帝[18]看。黄帝觉得这方法比
绳子好得多。于是他召集[19]
了天下的首领[20]，要他们把
这些图形带回去给人们。
人们用了这些图形以后，
可以记住更多的东西了。慢慢
地，这些图形就成了我们
今天的汉字了。

世界上的东西
都有自己的特征

這些圖形成了我們今天的漢字

這些特徵記下來，不就能代表[13]不同的東西了嗎？

　　然後，<u>倉頡</u>開始認真地觀察起周圍[14]的東西來，他發現[15]太陽是圓圓的，就用一個圓〇來代表太陽；月亮是彎彎的，那就畫一個彎（〕）吧，山是⊥，小河是≈。就這樣，<u>倉頡</u>畫出了越來越多的圖形[16]，他還發現把這些圖形組合[17]在一起，還可以表達更多的意思。

　　<u>倉頡</u>把這些圖形拿去給黃帝[18]看。黃帝覺得這方法比繩子好得多。於是他召集[19]了天下的首領[20]，要他們把這些圖形帶回去給人們。人們用了這些圖形以後，可以記住更多的東西了。慢慢地，這些圖形就成了我們今天的漢字了。

Vocabulary List

	SIMPLIFIED CHARACTERS	TRADITIONAL CHARACTERS	PINYIN	PART OF SPEECH	ENGLISH DEFINITION
1	仓颉	倉頡	Cāng Jié	pn.	(the mythical inventor of Chinese script)
	造字	造字	zàozì	vo.	to coin new Chinese characters
2	发明	發明	fāmíng	v.	to invent
3	结	結	jié	n.	knot
4	记录	記錄	jìlù	v.	to record
5	鱼	魚	yú	n.	fish
6	下决心	下決心	xià juéxīn	vo.	to make up one's mind
7	脚印	腳印	jiǎoyìn	n.	footprint
8	猎人	獵人	lièrén	n.	hunter
9	鸡	雞	jī	n.	chicken
10	细	細	xì	adj.	slim
11	突然	突然	tūrán	adv.	suddenly
12	特征	特徵	tèzhēng	n.	characteristics, features
13	代表	代表	dàibiǎo	v.	to represent
14	周围	周圍	zhōuwéi	n.	surroundings
15	发现	發現	fāxiàn	v.	to discover
16	图形	圖形	túxíng	n.	patterns

	SIMPLIFIED CHARACTERS	TRADITIONAL CHARACTERS	PINYIN	PART OF SPEECH	ENGLISH DEFINITION
17	组合	組合	zǔhé	vc.	to compose
18	黄帝	黃帝	Huángdì	pn.	the Yellow Emperor
19	召集	召集	zhàojí	v.	to summon
20	首领	首領	shǒulǐng	n.	chief, leader

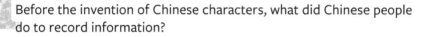

Questions

1 Before the invention of Chinese characters, what did Chinese people do to record information?

A. Draw pictures in the sand.
B. Tie strings into knots.
C. Draw pictures on their hands.
D. Tie bamboo into bundles.

2 What was Cang Jie's inspiration for his invention?

A. The scales on a fish.
B. The footprint of a mouse.
C. The bones of a fish.
D. The footprint of a chicken.

3 Cang Jie used a circle to represent the

A. sun.

B. moon.

C. eye.

D. earth.

4 Cang Jie used curvy lines to represent

A. mountains.

B. smoke.

C. rivers.

D. plants.

5 To whom did Cang Jie propose his idea?

A. A wise old man.

B. The old hunter.

C. The emperor.

D. The king.

DISCUSSION	**2.** Do you know how the Latin alphabet was invented? Before the alphabet, how did people in the West record information?
1. What is your favorite Chinese character and why?	**3.** While languages that use the Latin alphabet have root words, how can Chinese characters be broken down into different parts?

16

The God of Matchmaking

月下老人
月下老人

Yuè xià lǎo rén

为什么一个男人会遇见₁一个女人，爱上她并且跟她结婚呢？中国人相信₂，这些事情都是一位月下老人安排₃好的。

很久以前，有一个叫作韦固₄的年轻人。他常常在各地旅游，因此看见了很多又奇怪又有意思的事情。

有一个晚上，美丽的月亮升上了天空，韦固看见月亮这么美，决定出去走走。他走啊走啊，走到一棵大树旁边，看到一位老人坐在树下。老人的身边放了一个大口袋₅，正在认真地看一本又大又厚₆的书。

韦固想：真奇怪，这个老人为什么要在晚上坐在树下看书呢，他能看到什么呢？

于是，他走上前去，很客气地₇问："老人家，您在看什么呢？"

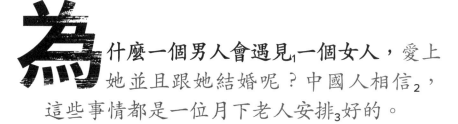

為什麼一個男人會遇見₁一個女人，愛上她並且跟她結婚呢？中國人相信₂，這些事情都是一位月下老人安排₃好的。

很久以前，有一個叫作韋固₄的年輕人。他常常在各地旅遊，因此看見了很多又奇怪又有意思的事情。

有一個晚上，美麗的月亮升上了天空，韋固看見月亮這麼美，決定出去走走。他走啊走啊，走到一棵大樹旁邊，看到一位老人坐在樹下。老人的身邊放了一個大口袋₅，正在認真地看一本又大又厚₆的書。

韋固想：真奇怪，這個老人為什麼要在晚上坐在樹下看書呢，他能看到什麼呢？

於是，他走上前去，很客氣地₇問："老人家，您在看什麼呢？"

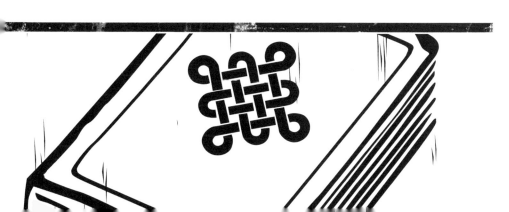

老人说："我手里的这本书可太重要了，它上面写着所有男男女女的婚姻[8]。你要是想知道你将来的妻子是谁，一看这本书就知道了。"

韦固又问："那您的大口袋里放着什么呢？"

老人打开口袋，原来里面放着许多又细又长的红线。老人说："这些红线是用来拴住[9]那些夫妻[10]的脚的。不管他们现在互相[11]认识不认识，也不管他们距离有多远，只要我把这根红线的一头拴在一个男人的脚上，再把另一头拴在一个女人的脚上，他们将来一定会结婚。"

韦固听了，觉得很好笑，就说："一根小小的红线怎么能拴住两个人呢？"

老人见韦固不相信，就说："好吧，我们一起来看看你将来的妻子是谁。"于是就在他的大书里找起来，"看，你的妻子就是这个穷人家的女儿。"

韦固一看，这个女孩子才五岁，家里很穷，两条眉毛[12]之间还有一条疤痕[13]。他怎么可能要这样的人做妻子呢？他觉得太好笑了，就跟老人说再见，然后回家了。

很快，韦固就忘了这件事情。

老人說："我手裡的這本書可太重要了，它上面寫著所有男男女女的婚姻[8]。你要是想知道你將來的妻子是誰，一看這本書就知道了。"

　　韋固又問："那您的大口袋裡放著什麼呢？"

　　老人打開口袋，原來裡面放著許多又細又長的紅線。老人說："這些紅線是用來拴住[9]那些夫妻[10]的腳的。不管他們現在互相[11]認識不認識，也不管他們距離有多遠，只要我把這根紅線的一頭拴在一個男人的腳上，再把另一頭拴在一個女人的腳上，他們將來一定會結婚。"

　　韋固聽了，覺得很好笑，就說："一根小小的紅線怎麼能拴住兩個人呢？"

　　老人見韋固不相信，就說："好吧，我們一起來看看你將來的妻子是誰。"於是就在他的大書裡找起來，"看，你的妻子就是這個窮人家的女兒。"

　　韋固一看，這個女孩子才五歲，家裡很窮，兩條眉毛[12]之間還有一條疤痕[13]。他怎麼可能要這樣的人做妻子呢？他覺得太好笑了，就跟老人說再見，然後回家了。

　　很快，韋固就忘了這件事情。

书上写着所有男男女女的婚姻

十四年后，<u>韦固</u>和一个有钱人家的女儿结了婚。他到了结婚那天才看到自己的妻子，发现她长得十分美丽，只是两条眉毛间有一条疤痕。<u>韦固</u>很吃惊[14]，忙问他的妻子。妻子说："我小的时候家里很穷，父母很早就死了，幸亏[15]有我的养父[16]把我养大，给我吃好的穿好的，还让我上学。"

<u>韦固</u>想起了十四年前月下老人的话，大吃一惊，原来男女姻缘真的是早就注定[17]了的！

十四年後，章固和一個有錢人家的女兒結了婚。他到了結婚那天才看到自己的妻子，發現她長得十分美麗，只是兩條眉毛間有一條疤痕。章固很吃驚14，忙問他的妻子。妻子說："我小的時候家裡很窮，父母很早就死了，幸虧15有我的養父16把我養大，給我吃好的穿好的，還讓我上學。"

章固想起了十四年前月下老人的話，大吃一驚，原來男女姻緣真的是早就注定17了的！

Vocabulary List

	SIMPLIFIED CHARACTERS	TRADITIONAL CHARACTERS	PINYIN	PART OF SPEECH	ENGLISH DEFINITION
1	遇见	遇見	yùjiàn	v.	to meet, to encounter
2	相信	相信	xiāngxìn	v.	to believe
3	安排	安排	ānpái	v.	to arrange
4	韦固	韋固	Wéi Gù	pn.	(name of a person)
5	口袋	口袋	kǒudài	n.	pocket
6	厚	厚	hòu	adj.	thick
7	客气地	客氣地	kèqi de	adv.	politely
8	婚姻	婚姻	hūnyīn	n.	marriage
9	拴住	拴住	shuānzhù	vc.	to fasten
10	夫妻	夫妻	fūqī	n.	husband and wife
11	互相	互相	hùxiāng	adv.	each other, mutually
12	眉毛	眉毛	méimao	n.	brow
13	疤痕	疤痕	bāhén	n.	scar

	SIMPLIFIED CHARACTERS	TRADITIONAL CHARACTERS	PINYIN	PART OF SPEECH	ENGLISH DEFINITION
14	吃惊	吃驚	chījīng	v.	to be shocked
15	幸亏	幸虧	xìngkuī	adv.	fortunately
16	养父	養父	yǎngfù	n.	foster father
17	注定	注定	zhùdìng	vc.	to decide by fate

Questions

1 When Wei Gu went out for a walk one night, he saw an old man

A. sitting under a tree, reading a large book.

B. sleeping under a tree.

C. gazing up at the moon.

D. loudly reciting poetry.

2 What important information did the old man have in his possession?

A. The names of all the men and women in the world.

B. The history of ancient China.

C. Records of all the marriages in the world.

D. Lists of future historical events.

3 Why did the old man have pieces of red thread in his pocket?

A. To keep his book bound together.

B. To fasten to the ring fingers of future husbands and wives.

C. To keep his book attached to the tree.

D. To fasten to the feet of future husbands and wives.

4 According to the old man, Wei Gu's future wife was a young girl

A. from a poor family and had a scar between her eyebrows.

B. from a wealthy family and had a beauty mark between her eyebrows.

C. who was well-known for the unique shape of her scar.

D. who was already matched with another future husband.

5 Wei Gu's wife was raised by

A. wealthy foster parents.

B. her foster father.

C. her poor family.

D. the old man.

DISCUSSION	**1.** Do you believe that marriage is predetermined by fate? Why or why not?

2. Online, research traditional marriages in China. Are they similar to traditional marriages in your culture? What unique Chinese wedding traditions do you find interesting?

生肖的故事

生肖的故事

17

The Story of the Twelve Zodiac Animals

生肖₁的故事

生肖₁的故事

Shēng xiào de gù shi

中国有十二个生肖，你知道他们的先后
顺序$_2$吗？是这样的：鼠$_3$、牛、虎、
兔、龙、蛇、马、羊$_4$、猴$_5$、鸡、狗、猪。
可是为什么小小的老鼠会排在第一位呢？这
其中有这样一个故事。

为了方便人们记住时间，天上的<u>玉帝</u>$_6$
选出了十二个动物，让每个动物代表一年。
可是哪个动物应该安排在第一，哪个动物
排在最后呢？这个问题让他很为难$_7$，于是
对这十二个动物说："你们来一次比赛吧，从
远远的那条河边跑到南天门$_8$，第一个跑到的
就代表第一年，第二个跑到的就是第二年，
第三个……你们觉得怎么样？"

动物们一听，个个都想做第一名。可是
老鼠却不太高兴。原来这十二个动物里面就
它最小，怎么得到第一呢？他想啊想啊，想出
了一个办法。

the story of the twelve zodiac animals   SIMPLIFIED   生肖的故事

中國有十二個生肖，你知道他們的先後順序₂嗎？是這樣的：鼠₃、牛、虎、兔、龍、蛇、馬、羊₄、猴₅、雞、狗、豬。可是為什麼小小的老鼠會排在第一位呢？這其中有這樣一個故事。

為了方便人們記住時間，天上的玉帝₆選出了十二個動物，讓每個動物代表一年。可是哪個動物應該安排在第一，哪個動物排在最後呢？這個問題讓他很為難₇，於是對這十二個動物說："你們來一次比賽吧，從遠遠的那條河邊跑到南天門₈，第一個跑到的就代表第一年，第二個跑到的就是第二年，第三個……你們覺得怎麼樣？"

動物們一聽，個個都想做第一名。可是老鼠卻不太高興。原來這十二個動物裡面就它最小，怎麼得到第一呢？他想啊想啊，想出了一個辦法。

鼠

比赛开始了，动物们谁也不让着谁。牛和虎又高大又强壮，它们跑得很快。兔子本来就很会跑，所以它也跑得很快。龙和蛇虽然没有脚，但是它们也很快，紧紧地 9 跟在后面。马、羊、猴、鸡、狗也都认真地跑着。小猪不爱运动，它跑在最后。可是小老鼠呢？谁也看不见它在哪儿。

很快，南天门就要到了，动物们跑得更快了。牛跑到老虎前面，成了第一个。他觉得自己一定会赢了，心里很高兴，赶快往终点 10 跑过去。可是，就在这时候，老鼠突然从牛角 11 上跳了下来，第一个跑到了终点。

因为老鼠知道自己跑得不快，所以一开始比赛，它就悄悄地躲在牛角后面。因为它很小，谁也没有看见它。就这样，老鼠成了十二生肖的第一名了。

比賽開始了，動物們誰也不讓著誰。牛和虎又高大又強壯，它們跑得很快。兔子本來就很會跑，所以它也跑得很快。龍和蛇雖然沒有腳，但是它們也很快，緊緊地[9]跟在後面。馬、羊、猴、雞、狗也都認真地跑著。小豬不愛運動，它跑在最後。可是小老鼠呢？誰也看不見它在哪兒。

很快，南天門就要到了，動物們跑得更快了。牛跑到老虎前面，成了第一個。他覺得自己一定會贏了，心裡很高興，趕快往終點[10]跑過去。可是，就在這時候，老鼠突然從牛角[11]上跳了下來，第一個跑到了終點。

因為老鼠知道自己跑得不快，所以一開始比賽，它就悄悄地躲在牛角後面。因為它很小，誰也沒有看見它。就這樣，老鼠成了十二生肖的第一名了。

Vocabulary List

	SIMPLIFIED CHARACTERS	TRADITIONAL CHARACTERS	PINYIN	PART OF SPEECH	ENGLISH DEFINITION
1	生肖	生肖	shēngxiào	n.	any of the twelve zodiac animals
2	先后顺序	先後順序	xiānhòu shùnxù	n.	order of sequencing
3	(老)鼠	(老)鼠	(lǎo)shǔ	n.	rat, mouse
4	羊	羊	yáng	n.	goat, sheep
5	猴(子)	猴(子)	hóu(zi)	n.	monkey
6	玉帝	玉帝	Yùdì	pn.	the Jade Emperor
7	为难	為難	wéinán	v.	to feel awkward
8	南天门	南天門	Nántiānmén	pn.	the Southern Heavenly Gate
9	紧紧地	緊緊地	jǐnjǐn de	adv.	tightly
10	终点	終點	zhōngdiǎn	n.	destination
11	牛角	牛角	niújiǎo	n.	ox horn

Questions

1 The Jade Emperor invited the twelve zodiac animals to participate in a race in order to determine

A. which animal was his favorite.
B. the order of the zodiac animals.
C. which animals would be included in the zodiac.
D. the names of the zodiac animals.

2 Which animal was not in the race?

A. The cat.
B. The rat.
C. The dog.
D. The rabbit.

3 The rat was unhappy about the race because

A. it could be eaten by any of the other animals.
B. the cat was participating in the race.
C. it was the smallest of all the competing animals.
D. the other animals got a head start.

4 The dragon and the snake were

A. in the lead throughout the race.
B. close behind the horse, sheep, and monkey.
C. close behind the ox, tiger, and rabbit.
D. disqualified from the race.

5 Which of the animals was trailing behind all the others?

A. The ox.

B. The sheep.

C. The snake.

D. The pig.

6 Which of the animals won first place?

A. The dragon.

B. The horse.

C. The rabbit.

D. The rat.

7 How did this animal win first place?

A. It rode on the back of the ox.

B. It jumped off the horn of the ox.

C. It hid in the mouth of the tiger.

D. It held onto the ears of the dog.

DISCUSSION

1. What is your Chinese zodiac animal? Using resources online, find out what its attributes are. Do you think you have these attributes? Why or why not?

2. What is your Western astrological sign? Do you have any of the characteristics attributed to it, and how does it compare to your Chinese zodiac animal?

畫龍點睛 画龙点睛

18

Dragon Eyes

画龙点睛[1]
畫龍點睛[1]

Huà lóng diǎn jīng

从前，有一位很有名的画家₂，名字叫张僧繇₃。他画山水人物₄、花草树木都画得非常好，就跟真的一样。人人都想要他画的画，但是张僧繇不轻易地₅为别人作画。

有一次，张僧繇到一座寺庙₆去游玩。他刚一进寺庙，就被庙里的和尚₇认出来了："哎呀，这不是有名的张僧繇吗？"这个和尚很早就想要张僧繇的画了，于是他赶快把最好的茶和最好的点心₈都拿出来，还带他参观₉自己的寺庙。

他们一起来到寺庙的大厅。和尚说："您看，这个大厅虽然很高很大，可是一幅₁₀画都没有。就请您在这墙上，为我画一幅画吧。"

张僧繇喝了他的好茶，吃了他的好点心，不好意思说"不"，就问："你想要我画什么呢？"

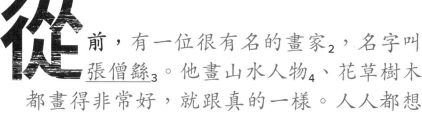

從前，有一位很有名的畫家₂，名字叫張僧繇₃。他畫山水人物₄、花草樹木都畫得非常好，就跟真的一樣。人人都想要他畫的畫，但是張僧繇不輕易地₅為別人作畫。

有一次，張僧繇到一座寺廟₆去遊玩。他剛一進寺廟，就被廟裡的和尚₇認出來了：“哎呀，這不是有名的張僧繇嗎？”這個和尚很早就想要張僧繇的畫了，於是他趕快把最好的茶和最好的點心₈都拿出來，還帶他參觀₉自己的寺廟。

他們一起來到寺廟的大廳。和尚說：“您看，這個大廳雖然很高很大，可是一幅₁₀畫都沒有。就請您在這牆上，為我畫一幅畫吧。”

張僧繇喝了他的好茶，吃了他的好點心，不好意思說“不”，就問：“你想要我畫什麼呢？”

和尚想：既然要画，就画一个大的东西。于是，他说："龙很大，那就画一条龙吧。请把这面墙都画满。"

张僧繇说"行！"他拿起画笔，不一会儿，就在墙上画了一条很大很大的龙。这条龙画得真好，看上去就跟真的一样。

和尚十分高兴，他对着墙上的龙看了好久，突然问："哎！这龙怎么没有眼睛？"

张僧繇说："我没有画它的眼睛，是怕它一有了眼睛，就变成一条真的龙了。"

和尚当然$_{11}$不相信，觉得张僧繇在骗$_{12}$他。于是他说："怎么会有这样的事儿呢？画出来的龙就是有了眼睛也不可能变成真的。请您还是把眼睛画上吧。"

张僧繇没有办法，只好拿起笔，给龙又画了两只眼睛。

还没等他放下笔，只听"轰$_{13}$"的一声，墙上的龙突然动了起来。它一甩尾巴$_{14}$，冲$_{15}$出了墙壁，往天上飞去了。

和尚一下子被吓呆$_{16}$了，等他明白$_{17}$过来，看见墙上的龙没有了，只剩下$_{18}$一个大洞。

和尚想：既然要畫，就畫一個大的東西。於是，他說："龍很大，那就畫一條龍吧。請把這面牆都畫滿。"

張僧繇說"行！"他拿起畫筆，不一會兒，就在牆上畫了一條很大很大的龍。這條龍畫得真好，看上去就跟真的一樣。

和尚十分高興，他對著牆上的龍看了好久，突然問："哎！這龍怎麼沒有眼睛？"

張僧繇說："我沒有畫它的眼睛，是怕它一有了眼睛，就變成一條真的龍了。"

和尚當然[11]不相信，覺得張僧繇在騙[12]他。於是他說："怎麼會有這樣的事兒呢？畫出來的龍就是有了眼睛也不可能變成真的。請您還是把眼睛畫上吧。"

張僧繇沒有辦法，只好拿起筆，給龍又畫了兩隻眼睛。

還沒等他放下筆，只聽"轟[13]"的一聲，牆上的龍突然動了起來。它一甩尾巴[14]，沖[15]出了牆壁，往天上飛去了。

和尚一下子被嚇呆[16]了，等他明白[17]過來，看見牆上的龍沒有了，只剩下[18]一個大洞。

TRADITIONAL 畫龍點睛 dragon eyes 157

Vocabulary List

	SIMPLIFIED CHARACTERS	TRADITIONAL CHARACTERS	PINYIN	PART OF SPEECH	ENGLISH DEFINITION
1	画龙	畫龍	huà lóng	vo.	to paint a dragon
	点	點	diǎn	v.	to touch on very briefly (as in painting with a brush)
	睛	睛	jīng	n.	eyes
2	画家	畫家	huàjiā	n.	artist, painter
3	张僧繇	張僧繇	Zhāng Sēngyáo	pn.	(name of a person)
4	人物	人物	rénwù	n.	people, figures
5	轻易地	輕易地	qīngyì de	adv.	easily
6	寺庙	寺廟	sìmiào	n.	temple
7	和尚	和尚	héshàng	n.	Buddhist monk
8	点心	點心	diǎnxin	n.	refreshments
9	参观	參觀	cānguān	v.	to visit
10	幅	幅	fú	mw.	(measure word for pictures)
11	当然	當然	dāngrán	adv.	certainly
12	骗	騙	piàn	v.	to lie, to deceive
13	轰	轟	hōng	on.	bang, boom
14	甩尾巴	甩尾巴	shuǎi wěiba	vo.	to swing one's tail

	SIMPLIFIED CHARACTERS	TRADITIONAL CHARACTERS	PINYIN	PART OF SPEECH	ENGLISH DEFINITION
15	冲	沖	chōng	v.	to dash
16	吓呆	嚇呆	xiàdāi	vc.	to be scared stiff
17	明白	明白	míngbai	v.	to understand, to realize
18	剩下	剩下	shèngxià	vc.	to be left over

Questions

1 Which of these was the artist Zhang Sengyao not originally known for painting?

A. Dragons
B. Mountains
C. Water
D. People

2 What did the monk do in the hope that Zhang Sengyao would paint him a picture in return?

A. He served Zhang Sengyao a modest meal of vegetables and porridge.
B. He served Zhang Sengyao his best tea and refreshments, then showed him around the temple.
C. He offered his best tea and refreshments to a shrine on behalf of Zhang Sengyao.
D. He gave Zhang Sengyao the only painting in his temple.

3 What did Zhang Sengyao purposely leave out of his painting?

A. The dragon's feet.

B. The dragon's eyes.

C. His name.

D. The date.

4 What happened when Zhang Sengyao reluctantly added what he had originally left out?

A. The monk thought there was a real dragon on the wall and he ran away.

B. The dragon came to life and attacked Zhang Sengyao and the monk.

C. Ye Gong visited the temple and asked to buy the painting.

D. The dragon came to life and flew up into the air.

5 What can the title of this story be best used to describe?

A. Leaving a masterpiece unfinished.

B. Taking a bribe.

C. Adding the crucial finishing touches.

D. Getting away with doing the bare minimum.

DISCUSSION

1. Do you think that Zhang Sengyao should have given in to the monk's final request? Why or why not?

2. How do you think the story "Drawing a Snake and Adding Feet" (画蛇添足 / 畫蛇添足) is similar to or different from this story? If needed, use Story 3 of *Tales and Traditions*, Volume 1 or resources online for reference.

19

Little Nezha Fights the Great Dragon King

哪吒闹海₁
哪吒鬧海₁

Nézhā nào hǎi

从前，有一位将军叫<u>李靖</u>₂，他已经有了两个儿子，现在又有了第三个儿子，叫<u>哪吒</u>。这个小儿子跟大家不一样。他出生以前，就在妈妈的身体里睡了三年。他出生的那天，大家都很高兴。可是，他一生下来，不是一个宝宝₃，而是一个红色的大肉球。他爸爸一看，觉得这一定是个妖怪，就拿起剑₄向那个肉球砍去。"啪₅"的一声，球分开了，里面躺着一个可爱的小男孩，这就是<u>哪吒</u>了。全家人看到这小男孩，都很喜欢，想去抱他，可是爸爸不高兴，他说："这一定是个妖怪，我要杀₆了他！"

就在这时候，一位天上的神仙出现了。他对<u>李靖</u>说："这个孩子将来会很有名，我要

<big>從</big>前，有一位將軍叫<u>李靖</u>₂，他已經
有了兩個兒子，現在又有了第三個
兒子，叫<u>哪吒</u>。這個小兒子跟大家不
一樣。他出生以前，就在媽媽的身體裡睡
了三年。他出生的那天，大家都很高興。
可是，他一生下來，不是一個寶寶₃，而
是一個紅色的大肉球。他爸爸一看，覺得
這一定是個妖怪，就拿起劍₄向那個肉球
砍去。"啪₅"的一聲，球分開了，裡面躺
著一個可愛的小男孩，這就是<u>哪吒</u>了。
全家人看到這小男孩，都很喜歡，想去抱
他，可是爸爸不高興，他說："這一定是個
妖怪，我要殺₆了他！"

就在這時候，一位天上的神仙出現
了。他對<u>李靖</u>說："這個孩子將來會很
有名，我要他做我的學生。"他送給<u>哪吒</u>三
樣東西：一是風火輪₇，踏₈上這隻輪子，

他做我的学生。"他送给哪吒三样东西：一是风火轮$_7$，踏$_8$上这只轮子，就能跑得比风还快；二是乾坤圈$_9$，亮闪闪的$_{10}$，拿在手上，什么样的敌人$_{11}$都能打败；三是混天绫$_{12}$，这块红色的布穿在身上很漂亮，还能保护哪吒不受伤。全家人听了太乙真人$_{13}$的话都很高兴，只有他的爸爸不相信，所以一直不喜欢他。

很快，哪吒七岁了，长得又聪明又可爱。有一天，他去东海游泳。他跳进水里，把身上的混天绫脱下来，放在水里洗了一下。这一洗可不得了，海水咆哮$_{14}$起来，一下就把海里龙宫的屋顶$_{15}$打翻$_{16}$了。住在龙宫里的东海龙王见屋顶没了，十分生气，他游出水面，对哪吒大喊道："你是谁家的孩子，怎么敢在我的大海里撒野$_{17}$？"

哪吒说："对不起，我真的不知道我的混天绫有这么大的力量$_{18}$，弄坏$_{19}$了你的房子。请你原谅$_{20}$我吧。"

龙王当然不答应$_{21}$，他对着哪吒又喊又骂$_{22}$。

哪吒越听越生气，他拿起混天绫，在水里抖$_{23}$了起来。每抖一下都带来了大地震$_{24}$，龙宫在水里摇摇晃晃$_{25}$，马上就要塌了。龙王一看，更生气了，他冲上来要打哪吒。哪吒就能跑得比風還快；二是乾坤圈[9]，亮閃閃的[10]，拿在手上，什麼樣的敵人[11]都能打敗；三是混天綾[12]，這塊紅色的布穿在身上很漂亮，還能保護哪吒不受傷。全家人聽了太乙真人[13]的話都很高興，只有他的爸爸不相信，所以一直不喜歡他。

很快，哪吒七歲了，長得又聰明又可愛。有一天，他去東海游泳。他跳進水裡，把身上的混天綾脫下來，放在水裡洗了一下。這一洗可不得了，海水咆哮[14]起來，一下就把海裡龍宮的屋頂[15]打翻[16]了。住在龍宮裡的東海龍王見屋頂沒了，十分生氣，他游出水面，對哪吒大喊道："你是誰家的孩子，怎麼敢在我的大海裡撒野[17]？"

哪吒說："對不起，我真的不知道我的混天綾有這麼大的力量[18]，弄壞[19]了你的房子。請你原諒[20]我吧。"

龍王當然不答應[21]，他對著哪吒又喊又罵[22]。

哪吒越聽越生氣，他拿起混天綾，在水裡抖[23]了起來。每抖一下都帶來了大地震[24]，龍宮在水裡搖搖晃晃[25]，馬上就要塌了。龍王一看，更生氣了，他沖上來要打哪吒。哪吒一抬手，手上的乾坤圈正好打在龍王頭上，一下子就把龍王打倒了。

龙宫在水里

摇摇晃晃

一抬手，手上的乾坤圈正好打在龙王头上，一下子就把龙王打倒了。看见龙王被打倒了，哪吒马上踏上风火轮，飞快地回家了。

没了房子又受了伤的龙王气极了，他一边追赶哪吒，一边念起咒语26，大海的水一下子就涨起来了，飞快地向哪吒的城市淹了过去。城里的人看见了，都大哭起来说，"我们这一下全完了，都要被淹死了！"

李靖一看，大骂哪吒："你这个畜牲27，我就知道你一定会给我们带来厄运28，我真应该早就把你杀了！"

哪吒看见自己给人们带来了这么大的麻烦，非常难过，就对父亲说："别担心，是我带来的麻烦，就让我来解决29吧。"

于是，他找到龙王，对他说："龙王，你不要淹了我的城市。是我弄坏了你的房子，又打伤30了你，现在就用我的生命来还给你吧。"

看見龍王被打倒了，哪吒馬上踏上風火輪，飛快地回家了。

沒了房子又受了傷的龍王氣極了，他一邊追趕哪吒，一邊念起咒語₂₆，大海的水一下子就漲起來了，飛快地向哪吒的城市淹了過去。城裡的人看見了，都大哭起來說，"我們這一下全完了，都要被淹死了！"

李靖一看，大罵哪吒："你這個畜牲₂₇，我就知道你一定會給我們帶來厄運₂₈，我真應該早就把你殺了！"

哪吒看見自己給人們帶來了這麼大的麻煩，非常難過，就對父親說："別擔心，是我帶來的麻煩，就讓我來解決₂₉吧。"

於是，他找到龍王，對他說："龍王，你不要淹了我的城市。是我弄壞了你的房子，又打傷₃₀了你，現在就用我的生命來還給你吧。"

說完，他拿出劍自殺₃₁了。

用我的生命來還給你

说完，他拿出剑自杀31了。

龙王见哪吒死了，就让海水退了回去。城里的人得救32了！他们看到哪吒那么小的孩子，就为大家牺牲33了自己，都十分感动。

这时候，太乙真人来了。他带着哪吒的身体回到天上，救活了他，教他更多的本领34。后来，哪吒成了有名的大将军。他踏着风火轮，拿着乾坤圈，穿着混天绫，哪里有妖怪他就到哪里去，把妖怪打败。中国人都很喜欢哪吒，他的故事到处流传35。每年四月八日和九日，人们都会纪念他，庆祝他的生日，感谢他给人们做了那么多好事。

龍王見哪吒死了，就讓海水退了回去。城裡的人得救32了！他們看到哪吒那麼小的孩子，就為大家犧牲33了自己，都十分感動。

這時候，太乙真人來了。他帶著哪吒的身體回到天上，救活了他，教他更多的本領34。後來，哪吒成了有名的大將軍。他踏著風火輪，拿著乾坤圈，穿著混天綾，哪裡有妖怪他就到哪裡去，把妖怪打敗。中國人都很喜歡哪吒，他的故事到處流傳35。每年四月八日和九日，人們都會紀念他，慶祝他的生日，感謝他給人們做了那麼多好事。

Vocabulary List

	SIMPLIFIED CHARACTERS	TRADITIONAL CHARACTERS	PINYIN	PART OF SPEECH	ENGLISH DEFINITION
1	闹海	鬧海	nào hǎi	vo.	to fight dragons in the sea
2	李靖	李靖	Lǐ Jìng	pn.	(name of a person)
3	宝宝	寶寶	bǎobao	n.	baby
4	剑	劍	jiàn	n.	sword
5	啪	啪	pā	on.	(sound of popping or bursting)
6	杀	殺	shā	v.	to kill
7	风火轮	風火輪	fēnghuǒ lún	n.	wind-fire wheels
8	踏	踏	tà	v.	to step on
9	乾坤圈	乾坤圈	qiánkūn quān	n.	universe ring
10	亮闪闪的	亮閃閃的	liàngshǎn shǎn de	adj.	shining
11	敌人	敵人	dírén	n.	enemy
12	混天绫	混天綾	hùn tiān líng	n.	celestial red silk sash

	SIMPLIFIED CHARACTERS	TRADITIONAL CHARACTERS	PINYIN	PART OF SPEECH	ENGLISH DEFINITION
13	太乙真人	太乙真人	Tàiyǐ Zhēnrén	pn.	(name of a Daoist immortal)
14	咆哮	咆哮	páoxiào	v.	to roar, to thunder
15	屋顶	屋頂	wūdǐng	n.	roof
16	打翻	打翻	dǎfān	vc.	to overturn
17	撒野	撒野	sāyě	v.	to act wildly
18	力量	力量	lìliang	n.	strength
19	弄坏	弄壞	nònghuài	vc.	to damage
20	原谅	原諒	yuánliàng	v.	to forgive
21	答应	答應	dāying	v.	to agree
22	骂	罵	mà	v.	to scold, to berate
23	抖	抖	dǒu	v.	to shake
24	地震	地震	dìzhèn	n.	earthquake

	SIMPLIFIED CHARACTERS	TRADITIONAL CHARACTERS	PINYIN	PART OF SPEECH	ENGLISH DEFINITION
25	摇摇晃晃	搖搖晃晃	yáoyáo huànghuàng	v.	to tremble
26	咒语	咒語	zhòuyǔ	n.	curse
27	畜牲	畜牲	chùsheng	n.	beast, dirty swine
28	厄运	厄運	èyùn	n.	adversity, misfortune
29	解决	解決	jiějué	v.	to solve
30	打伤	打傷	dǎshāng	vc.	to injure
31	自杀	自殺	zìshā	v.	to commit suicide
32	得救	得救	déjiù	v.	to be rescued
33	牺牲	犧牲	xīshēng	v.	to sacrifice
34	本领	本領	běnlǐng	n.	skills
35	流传	流傳	liúchuán	v.	to circulate, to spread

Questions

1 What was unusual about the birth of Li Jing's son Nezha?

A. He slept for three years after he was born.

B. He slept for three years before he was born.

C. He was born as an immortal.

D. He was born with a sword in his hand.

2 Li Jing slashed the ball of flesh surrounding Nezha because he was

A. desperate to save his son's life.

B. eager to see his new baby boy.

C. certain that his son was a monster.

D. scared of what might happen to his son.

3 Which of these did Nezha not receive from the immortal?

A. A red silk sash.

B. A universe ring.

C. A pair of wind-fire wheels.

D. A bow with fire-tipped arrows.

4 Why did the Dragon King become angry and attack Nezha?

A. Nezha went swimming in the East Sea, which was the Dragon King's territory.

B. Nezha washed his red silk sash in the water, which overturned the Dragon King's roof.

C. Nezha accidentally struck the Dragon King with his universe ring.

D. Nezha destroyed the Dragon King's roof when he dove into the water.

5 How did Li Jing react when the Dragon King flooded the city?

A. He was worried for Nezha's safety.

B. He changed his mind about Nezha being a monster.

C. He said that he should have killed Nezha earlier.

D. He wanted to join Nezha and fight against the Dragon King.

6 How did Nezha stop the Dragon King from flooding the city?

A. He claimed responsibility for damaging the Dragon King's roof and sacrificed his life.

B. He defeated the Dragon King by using the weapons he received from the immortal.

C. He defeated the Dragon King with the help of his father.

D. He caused a series of earthquakes that severely injured the Dragon King.

7 What happened to Nezha after saving the city from the flood?

A. He was revived by the immortal.

B. He became a famous general.

C. He defeated many other monsters.

D. All of the above.

DISCUSSION	**1.** Nezha is an important mythological figure who appears in classics such as *Journey to the West* (西游记 / 西遊記) and is referenced in popular culture. Why do you think Nezha is such a revered figure in China?

2. Are there similar figures from other mythologies who are still referenced to this day? How are such figures similar to or different from Nezha?

IV

Classic Tales of Love and Romance
第四章　　愛情故事
第四章　　愛情故事

20

Beauty in the Painting

画中人
畫中人

Huà zhōng rén

很久以前，有一个书生₁，家里很穷。他的父母很早就死了，只给他留下了一间破房子₂和一张画，画上有一位姑娘₃。那姑娘很美丽，眼睛好像会说话。

这个书生很爱学习，每天晚上都在家里读书。可是，他很穷，没有钱买书。所以他每天都得出去工作，赚钱买书和吃的东西。

他每天出门以前，都会看看那张画，然后对画中的姑娘说："再见！"画中的姑娘也看着他，好像听得懂他的话。

有一天，他又累又饿，想赶快回家做饭吃。可是，一走进家里，他就看见房子打扫得干干净净，衣服也洗好了，整整齐齐地₄放在床上，而且，桌子上还放着热气腾腾₅的饭菜。

很久以前，有一個書生[1]，家裡很窮。他的父母很早就死了，只給他留下了一間破房子[2]和一張畫，畫上有一位姑娘[3]。那姑娘很美麗，眼睛好像會說話。

這個書生很愛學習，每天晚上都在家裡讀書。可是，他很窮，沒有錢買書。所以他每天都得出去工作，賺錢買書和吃的東西。

他每天出門以前，都會看看那張畫，然後對畫中的姑娘說："再見！"畫中的姑娘也看著他，好像聽得懂他的話。

有一天，他又累又餓，想趕快回家做飯吃。可是，一走進家裡，他就看見房子打掃得干干淨淨，衣服也洗好了，整整齊齊地[4]放在床上，而且，桌子上還放著熱氣騰騰[5]的飯菜。

书生很吃惊，他想：这是谁做的呢？谁来帮助我呢？他在房子里到处找，可是一个人也没找到。最后，他对自己说："算了，还是先吃饭吧。"他高高兴兴地吃了饭，一边说："真好吃！"，一边走到床边，躺下去好好儿睡了一觉。

从这天开始，连着₆好几天，每天都是这样。书生问了邻居张先生，李小姐，他们都说不知道，不是他们做的。书生觉得奇怪极了，他决定想个办法找到这个人。

这天早上，他像平常一样，对着那张画说："再见！"就出门了。

可是，他一会儿就回来了，躲在房子外面，往里面看。

突然，墙上的那张画动了起来，然后画上那个美丽的姑娘从上面走了下来。她到处看了看，就开始扫地，做饭，收拾₇房子。

书生又高兴又吃惊，他跑进房子里，对着那个姑娘说："姑娘，请问你是谁？你怎么从画上下来了？你为什么要来帮助我呢？"

那姑娘也很吃惊，她红着脸，小声地₈说："我是天上的仙女₉，因为王母娘娘不喜欢我，就把我变成了画上的人。可是，書生很吃驚，他想：這是誰做的呢？誰來幫助我呢？他在房子裡到處找，可是一個人也沒找到。最後，他對自己說："算了，還是先吃飯吧。"他高高興興地吃了飯，一邊說："真好吃！"，一邊走到床邊，躺下去好好兒睡了一覺。

從這天開始，連著[6]好幾天，每天都是這樣。書生問了鄰居張先生，李小姐，他們都說不知道，不是他們做的。書生覺得奇怪極了，他決定想個辦法找到這個人。

這天早上，他像平常一樣，對著那張畫說："再見！"就出門了。

可是，他一會兒就回來了，躲在房子外面，往裡面看。

突然，牆上的那張畫動了起來，然後畫上那個美麗的姑娘從上面走了下來。她到處看了看，就開始掃地，做飯，收拾[7]房子。

書生又高興又吃驚，他跑進房子裡，對著那個姑娘說："姑娘，請問你是誰？你怎麼從畫上下來了？你為什麼要來幫助我呢？"

那姑娘也很吃驚，她紅著臉，小聲地[8]說："我是天上的仙女[9]，因為王母娘娘

美丽的姑娘

从画上走了下来

你每天都看着我，跟我说话，慢慢地我就可以动了。我看见你一个人过得很辛苦，就早上从画上走下来帮助你，晚上再回到画上去。"

书生听了，高兴极了，他拉着她的手，说："那你就留下来吧，不要再回到画上去了。我们在一起生活，好吗？"

姑娘点了点头，同意了。就这样，他们结婚了，从此快快乐乐地生活在一起。

不喜歡我，就把我變成了畫上的人。可是，你每天都看著我，跟我說話，慢慢地我就可以動了。我看見你一個人過得很辛苦，就早上從畫上走下來幫助你，晚上再回到畫上去。"

書生聽了，高興極了，他拉著她的手，說："那你就留下來吧，不要再回到畫上去了。我們在一起生活，好嗎？"

姑娘點了點頭，同意了。就這樣，他們結婚了，從此快快樂樂地生活在一起。

他們快快樂樂地 生活在一起

Vocabulary List

	SIMPLIFIED CHARACTERS	TRADITIONAL CHARACTERS	PINYIN	PART OF SPEECH	ENGLISH DEFINITION
1	书生	書生	shūshēng	n.	student, scholar
2	房子	房子	fángzi	n.	house
3	姑娘	姑娘	gūniang	n.	girl, lady
4	整整齐齐地	整整齊齊地	zhěngzhěng qíqi de	adv.	neatly
5	热气腾腾	熱氣騰騰	rèqì téngténg	adj.	piping hot
6	连着	連著	liánzhe	v.	to be continuous
7	收拾	收拾	shōushi	v.	to clean up
8	小声地	小聲地	xiǎoshēng de	adv.	softly (in tone), quietly
9	仙女	仙女	xiānnǚ	n.	fairy maiden

Questions

1 What was unique about the eyes of the girl in the student's painting?

A. They seemed to follow him when he walked around the room.

B. They seemed to be able to speak.

C. They were left unfinished so that she would not come to life.

D. They would blink whenever he was not looking.

2 What did the student do every day before leaving the house?

A. He said goodbye to the girl in the painting.

B. He said hello to the girl in the painting.

C. He waited for the girl in the painting to say goodbye to him.

D. He waited for the girl in the painting to say hello to him.

3 Which of the following did the student not find when he returned home?

A. A clean house.

B. Washed clothes.

C. A hot meal on the table.

D. A blank painting.

4 What did the student do in order to find out who was doing his chores for him?

A. He did not say goodbye to the painting before leaving his house.

B. He did not dust off the painting like he used to.

C. He hid outside the house and peered inside.

D. He hid inside the house and waited.

5 The Heavenly Queen put the girl inside the painting because

    A. the Heavenly Queen did not like her.

    B. the girl had no other place to live.

    C. the Heavenly Queen did not want her to fall in love.

    D. the girl had committed a crime.

6 What did the student do every day that helped the girl slowly begin to move again?

    A. He made her a hot meal.

    B. He dusted off the painting.

    C. He looked at her and spoke to her.

    D. He wrote letters to her.

7 When the student asked the girl in the painting to marry him,

    A. the Heavenly Queen forbid them from seeing each other.

    B. the girl agreed and they lived happily ever after.

    C. the girl agreed but had to return to the painting every night.

    D. the Heavenly Queen gave her permission and lifted the curse.

DISCUSSION

1. Can you draw any parallels between this fairytale and those in your own cultural tradition?

2. Online, research 王母娘娘. How is she depicted differently in this story from other stories?

21

The Love Story of a Fish Spirit

鲤鱼精₁的故事
鯉魚精₁的故事

Lǐ yú jīng de gù shi

从前，有一个富人₂，叫金宠。他有一个女儿，叫牡丹，她又聪明又漂亮。金宠有一个老朋友，他有一个儿子，叫张珍。张珍长得很好看，也很友好，他很喜欢读书。

金宠觉得张珍读书读得很好，以后一定能做大官的。所以，他就对张珍的父亲说，自己很喜欢张珍，要他和牡丹小姐订婚₃。张珍的父亲看到了牡丹，也很喜欢她，就高兴地同意了。

可是过了不久，张珍的父亲突然生病，很快就死了。过了几个月，他的母亲也生病死了。就这样，张珍没有了父母，没有了钱，也没有了家。他到金宠家去，希望得到他们的帮助。金宠见了他，说："好久不见，你怎么样？"张珍听了，哭着说："我的爸爸妈妈不久前₄都生病死了，现在家里只有我一个人。我一分钱都没有了。"

從前，有一個富人₂，叫金寵。他有一個女兒，叫牡丹，她又聰明又漂亮。金寵有一個老朋友，他有一個兒子，叫張珍。張珍長得很好看，也很友好，他很喜歡讀書。

金寵覺得張珍讀書讀得很好，以後一定能做大官的。所以，他就對張珍的父親說，自己很喜歡張珍，要他和牡丹小姐訂婚₃。張珍的父親看到了牡丹，也很喜歡她，就高興地同意了。

可是過了不久，張珍的父親突然生病，很快就死了。過了幾個月，他的母親也生病死了。就這樣，張珍沒有了父母，沒有了錢，也沒有了家。他到金寵家去，希望得到他們的幫助。金寵見了他，說："好久不見，你怎麼樣？"張珍聽了，哭著說："我的爸爸媽媽不久前₄都生病死了，現在家裡只有我一個人。我一分錢都沒有了。"

金宠听说张珍的父亲母亲都死了，家里变得很穷了，就很不高兴地说："你不在家里读书，来我这里做什么？"张珍说："我父母都死了，一个人在家里很难过，所以来找牡丹小姐。"

金宠一听，更不高兴了，什么话也没说就走了。张珍没办法，就自己去找牡丹。可是牡丹也和她爸爸一样，她冷冷地$_5$说："我也帮不了你什么忙。现在你来了，就住在我们家湖边$_6$的小草棚$_7$子里，在那儿好好读书吧。"

张珍就住到那个草棚子里去了，可是草棚子又小又破，下雨的时候漏$_8$雨，下雪的时候漏雪。张珍的生活虽然这么辛苦，但他每天都认真读书，准备参加皇家考试$_9$。

张珍读书读累了的时候，就走出草棚，去湖边走一走。湖里有一条美丽的红鲤鱼，张珍很喜欢它，就常常坐在湖边对着它说话，说自己以前的事情，说他很想父亲母亲，还说他每天在书上读到了些什么。

张珍不知道，这条红鲤鱼并不是真正的鱼，而是一个鲤鱼精。她看见张珍每天认真读书，很感动，又听了张珍的故事，就慢慢地爱上了他。看到牡丹和她爸爸都对张珍不友好，她就想好好帮助他。

金寵聽說張珍的父親母親都死了，家裡變得很窮了，就很不高興地說：“你不在家裡讀書，來我這裡做什麼？”張珍說：“我父母都死了，一個人在家裡很難過，所以來找牡丹小姐。”

金寵一聽，更不高興了，什麼話也沒說就走了。張珍沒辦法，就自己去找牡丹。可是牡丹也和她爸爸一樣，她冷冷地$_5$說：“我也幫不了你什麼忙。現在你來了，就住在我們家湖邊$_6$的小草棚$_7$子裡，在那兒好好讀書吧。”

張珍就住到那個草棚子裡去了，可是草棚子又小又破，下雨的時候漏$_8$雨，下雪的時候漏雪。張珍的生活雖然這麼辛苦，但他每天都認真讀書，准備參加皇家考試$_9$。

張珍讀書讀累了的時候，就走出草棚，去湖邊走一走。湖裡有一條美麗的紅鯉魚，張珍很喜歡它，就常常坐在湖邊對著它說話，說自己以前的事情，說他很想父親母親，還說他每天在書上讀到了些什麼。

張珍不知道，這條紅鯉魚並不是真正的魚，而是一個鯉魚精。她看見張珍每天認真讀書，很感動，又聽了張珍的故事，就慢慢地愛上了他。看到牡丹和她爸爸都對張珍不友好，她就想好好幫助他。

于是，她把自己变成牡丹小姐，每天都去看张珍，给他做饭，洗衣服，扫地。张珍以为这是真正的牡丹小姐，高兴极了，也更加[10]认真读书了。

三年过去了，张珍去参加考试，得了第一名，做了大官。张珍赶快回到金宠家，去感谢牡丹小姐。可是，他的面前出现[11]了两个一模一样[12]的牡丹小姐，因为那个真正的牡丹小姐看见张珍做了大官，也赶快来找他，说自己很爱他。然后，两位牡丹小姐打了起来，都说自己爱张珍，要跟他结婚。

张珍大吃一惊，又不知道哪个是真牡丹，哪个是假[13]牡丹。就在这时候，天上的观音娘娘[14]出现了，她对张珍说，"别急，我知道谁是真的，谁是假的。"然后她指[15]着鲤鱼精说："她是假的，但她是那个一直帮助你的人。在你最困难[16]的时候，她一直爱着你，没有抛弃[17]过你。"

张珍听了观音娘娘的话，很感动，他拉起了鲤鱼精的手，说："谢谢你一直帮助我。我爱的人就是你。"就这样，张珍和鲤鱼精结婚了。从此以后，他们生活在一起，过得很快乐。

於是，她把自己變成牡丹小姐，每天都去看張珍，給他做飯，洗衣服，掃地。張珍以為這是真正的牡丹小姐，高興極了，也更加[10]認真讀書了。

三年過去了，張珍去參加考試，得了第一名，做了大官。張珍趕快回到金寵家，去感謝牡丹小姐。可是，他的面前出現[11]了兩個一模一樣[12]的牡丹小姐，因為那個真正的牡丹小姐看見張珍做了大官，也趕快來找他，說自己很愛他。然後，兩位牡丹小姐打了起來，都說自己愛張珍，要跟他結婚。

張珍大吃一驚，又不知道哪個是真牡丹，哪個是假[13]牡丹。就在這時候，天上的觀音娘娘[14]出現了，她對張珍說，"別急，我知道誰是真的，誰是假的。"然後她指[15]著鯉魚精說："她是假的，但她是那個一直幫助你的人。在你最困難[16]的時候，她一直愛著你，沒有拋棄[17]過你。"

張珍聽了觀音娘娘的話，很感動，他拉起了鯉魚精的手，說："謝謝你一直幫助我。我愛的人就是你。"就這樣，張珍和鯉魚精結婚了。從此以後，他們生活在一起，過得很快樂。

Vocabulary List

	SIMPLIFIED CHARACTERS	TRADITIONAL CHARACTERS	PINYIN	PART OF SPEECH	ENGLISH DEFINITION
1	鲤鱼	鯉魚	lǐyú	n.	carp
	精	精	jīng	n.	spirit
2	富人	富人	fùrén	n.	rich person
3	订婚	訂婚	dìnghūn	v.	to be betrothed
4	不久前	不久前	bùjiǔ qián	adv.	a while ago
5	冷冷地	冷冷地	lěnglěng de	adv.	coldly
6	湖边	湖邊	hú biān	n.	lakeside, by the lake
7	草棚	草棚	cǎo péng	n.	straw mat shed
8	漏	漏	lòu	v.	to leak
9	皇家考试	皇家考試	huángjiā kǎoshì	n.	Imperial Examination
10	更加	更加	gèngjiā	adv.	even more
11	出现	出現	chūxiàn	v.	to appear
12	一模一样	一模一樣	yīmú yīyàng	adj.	exactly the same
13	假	假	jiǎ	adj.	false
14	观音娘娘	觀音娘娘	Guānyīn Niángniang	pn.	Bodhisattva Guanyin
15	指	指	zhǐ	v.	to point at
16	困难	困難	kùnnan	adj.	difficult
17	抛弃	拋棄	pāoqì	v.	to abandon

Questions

1 What did Jin Chong and his old friend agree upon?

A. Zhang Zhen and Lady Mudan were to be married.

B. Zhang Zhen would be adopted by Lady Mudan's family upon his father's death.

C. Zhang Zhen and Lady Mudan were to never be married.

D. Lady Mudan would be adopted by Zhang Zhen's family upon Jin Chong's death.

2 When Zhang Zhen's parents passed away, Jin Chong

A. welcomed him as his adopted son.

B. refused to allow Zhang Zhen to marry his daughter.

C. became angry and asked why Zhang Zhen was not studying.

D. refused to allow Zhang Zhen to visit his daughter.

3 When Zhang Zhen was tired from reading, he would sit by the lake and

A. talk to Lady Mudan about his past and what he was reading.

B. watch the carp swim.

C. talk to the carp about his past and what he was reading.

D. look at his reflection.

4 What did the fish spirit do for Zhang Zhen?

A. She helped him prepare for the Imperial Examination.

B. She cooked and cleaned for him.

C. She convinced Jin Chong to allow him to marry Lady Mudan.

D. She had Lady Mudan cook and clean for him.

5. What was the result of Zhang Zhen's Imperial Examination?

A. He received the highest score.

B. He failed and returned to Jin Chong's home for help.

C. He received the third-highest score.

D. He returned to Jin Chong's home to thank him for his help.

6. When Zhang Zhen returned to Jin Chong's home,

A. Jin Chong asked Zhang Zhen to marry his daughter.

B. Jin Chong no longer wanted Zhang Zhen to marry his daughter.

C. only the fish spirit wanted to marry Zhang Zhen.

D. both the fish spirit and Lady Mudan wanted to marry Zhang Zhen.

7. Who did Zhang Zhen choose to marry?

A. Bodhisattva Guanyin.

B. Lady Mudan.

C. The fish spirit.

D. Both Lady Mudan and the fish spirit.

DISCUSSION	**1.** Is there a moral (or two) to this story? Explain.

2. Online, research the Imperial Examination system in China. How did it influence Chinese culture, politics, and education? What do you think its legacy is today in modern China? Based on Zhang Zhen's performance on the exam, what do you think his rank was?

白蛇傳
白蛇传

22

Lady White Snake

白蛇传₁
白蛇傳₁

Bái shé zhuàn

杭州西湖是个很美丽的地方，那儿的风景美得就像画一样。那儿的天气也很好，所以每天都有很多人去玩儿。

有一天，突然两个漂亮的姑娘从西湖里面走了出来。看见她们的人都大吃一惊：人怎么能从水里走出来呢？她们怎么没淹死呢？大家不知道，这两个姑娘不是真正的人，她们是两个蛇精₂。一个是白蛇，叫白素贞；另一个是青蛇，叫小青。她们在峨嵋山上修炼₃了一千多年，变成了两个美丽的姑娘。这一天，她们看见西湖边有那么多人，就也下山来玩儿。

白素贞和小青玩儿得可高兴了，她们都不想回家了。可是，一会儿刮起₄了大风，下起了大雨。人们都赶快回家了。白素贞和小青正不知道怎么办，突然看见一位书生正拿着伞₅，在给她们遮雨₆。白素贞看见他这么友好，就很喜欢他。

杭州西湖是個很美麗的地方，那兒的風景美得就像畫一樣。那兒的天氣也很好，所以每天都有很多人去玩兒。

有一天，突然兩個漂亮的姑娘從西湖裡面走了出來。看見她們的人都大吃一驚：人怎麼能從水裡走出來呢？她們怎麼沒淹死呢？大家不知道，這兩個姑娘不是真正的人，她們是兩個蛇精2。一個是白蛇，叫白素貞；另一個是青蛇，叫小青。她們在峨嵋山上修煉3了一千多年，變成了兩個美麗的姑娘。這一天，她們看見西湖邊有那麼多人，就也下山來玩兒。

白素貞和小青玩兒得可高興了，她們都不想回家了。可是，一會兒颳起4了大風，下起了大雨。人們都趕快回家了。白素貞和小青正不知道怎麼辦，突然看見一位書生正拿著傘5，在給她們遮雨6。白素貞看見他這麼友好，就很喜歡他。

小青看见了书生，就对他说："谢谢您！请问您叫什么名字？"

那位书生笑着说："不客气。我叫许仙，我家就住在西湖边上。我看见下雨了，怕你们淋湿₇了衣服，就来给你们遮雨。"

白素贞和小青听了，都很感动。从这一天开始，他们常常一起在西湖边见面。很快，白素贞和许仙结婚了，在西湖边上住了下来，每天还忙着给人看病。邻居们都很喜欢他们，把白素贞叫作"白娘子"。可是，金山寺₈里的法海和尚很不高兴，因为大家有病都去找白娘子了，去他那儿烧香₉的人就少了很多。

有一天，法海和尚来到白娘子家，看见她正忙着给大家看病。他再一看，哎呀！这哪是什么白娘子，这不是白蛇精吗？

法海和尚决定不让白娘子给人们看病，也不让许仙再爱她。于是，他送了一瓶酒给许仙，要他跟白娘子一起喝。许仙不知道这个和尚是坏人，就跟白娘子一起把酒喝完了。白娘子喝了以后，很快就昏睡过去了。而且，她一睡着，就变回去了，成了一条大白蛇。许仙突然看见床上躺着一条大白蛇，吓得大叫一声，就昏死过去了。

<u>小青</u>看見了書生，就對他說："謝謝您！請問您叫什麼名字？"

　　那位書生笑著說："不客氣。我叫<u>許仙</u>，我家就住在西湖邊上。我看見下雨了，怕你們淋濕₇了衣服，就來給你們遮雨。"

　　<u>白素貞</u>和<u>小青</u>聽了，都很感動。從這一天開始，他們常常一起在西湖邊見面。很快，<u>白素貞</u>和<u>許仙</u>結婚了，在西湖邊上住了下來，每天還忙著給人看病。鄰居們都很喜歡他們，把<u>白素貞</u>叫作"<u>白娘子</u>"。可是，金山寺₈裡的<u>法海和尚</u>很不高興，因為大家有病都去找<u>白娘子</u>了，去他那兒燒香₉的人就少了很多。

　　有一天，<u>法海和尚</u>來到<u>白娘子</u>家，看見她正忙著給大家看病。他再一看，哎呀！這哪是什麼<u>白娘子</u>，這不是白蛇精嗎？

　　<u>法海和尚</u>決定不讓<u>白娘子</u>給人們看病，也不讓<u>許仙</u>再愛她。於是，他送了一瓶酒給<u>許仙</u>，要他跟<u>白娘子</u>一起喝。<u>許仙</u>不知道這個和尚是壞人，就跟<u>白娘子</u>一起把酒喝完了。<u>白娘子</u>喝了以後，很快就昏睡過去了。而且，她一睡著，就變回去了，成了一條大白蛇。<u>許仙</u>突然看見床上躺著一條大白蛇，嚇得大叫一聲，就昏死過去了。

白素贞醒了以后，看见许仙死了，大哭起来。为了救许仙，她和小青一起去偷仙草[10]。一路上她们很辛苦，遇到[11]了很多困难，最后终于把仙草偷到了。

白素贞和小青回到家里，把仙草放进许仙口里，许仙很快就醒过来了。许仙醒了以后，突然想起床上的大白蛇，心里怕极了，不想再跟白娘子在一起生活了。可是想到她救了自己，又很感动，他想："她对我那么好，虽然她是蛇精，我还是要爱她。"

可是，法海和尚又想了一个办法，他把许仙骗到他的金山寺里，对他说："你的白娘子是白蛇精变的，有一天她会把你吃下去的！"

许仙听了法海和尚的话，很不高兴，他说："我的白娘子对大家都很好，她常常给人看病，救了很多人。我昏死过去以后，她又去偷仙草，救了我的命。虽然她是蛇精，可是她比谁都好。而且，她已经怀孕[12]了，我就要做爸爸了，我可不要听你的坏话。"

法海和尚看见许仙不听他的话，就不让许仙回家，把他关[13]在金山寺里。白娘子不知道许仙到哪儿去了，很着急。她等呀等呀，一天、两天、三天……很多天过去了，许仙还是没有回来。

白素貞醒了以後，看見許仙死了，大哭起來。為了救許仙，她和小青一起去偷仙草₁₀。一路上她們很辛苦，遇到了很多困難，最後終於把仙草偷到了。

白素貞和小青回到家裡，把仙草放進許仙口裡，許仙很快就醒過來了。許仙醒了以後，突然想起床上的大白蛇，心裡怕極了，不想再跟白娘子在一起生活了。可是想到她救了自己，又很感動，他想："她對我那麼好，雖然她是蛇精，我還是要愛她。"

可是，法海和尚又想了一個辦法，他把許仙騙到他的金山寺裡，對他說："你的白娘子是白蛇精變的，有一天她會把你吃下去的！"

許仙聽了法海和尚的話，很不高興，他說："我的白娘子對大家都很好，她常常給人看病，救了很多人。我昏死過去以後，她又去偷仙草，救了我的命。雖然她是蛇精，可是她比誰都好。而且，她已經懷孕₁₂了，我就要做爸爸了，我可不要聽你的壞話。"

法海和尚看見許仙不聽他的話，就不讓許仙回家，把他關₁₃在金山寺裡。白娘子不知道許仙到哪兒去了，很著急。她等呀后来，白娘子听说许仙被法海和尚关起来了，就带着小青去金山寺，要法海和尚放许仙回家。法海和尚见了白娘子，冷冷地说："白蛇精，你还来找我！赶快回你的峨嵋山去吧。要不然，我可不客气了！"

白娘子见法海和尚就是不让许仙回家，就拔下头上的金钗，用手一划，前面就出现了一条大河，往金山寺淹过去。法海和尚看见大水就要淹到金山寺了，赶快脱下[14]他的袈裟[15]，让它变成一道长堤[16]，把水拦[17]在门外。白娘子的水高一尺，法海的堤就高一丈。就这样，白娘子的水再大，也淹不到金山寺。因为白娘子怀孕了，身体不好，很快就被法海打败了。打败白娘子以后，法海把她压在西湖边的雷峰塔下，要她永远见不到许仙，许仙也见不到她。可是，小青逃[18]回了峨眉山，在那儿又修炼了十几年，再回去找法海和尚。

找到法海和尚以后，小青跟他打了三天三夜，终于把他打败了。然后小青救出了许仙和孩子，又一起去救白娘子。就这样，许仙一家终于团圆了。从此，他们跟小青在一起，过着快乐的生活。

等呀，一天、兩天，三天……很多天過去了，<u>許仙</u>還是沒有回來。

後來，<u>白娘子</u>聽說<u>許仙</u>被<u>法海和尚</u>關起來了，就帶著<u>小青</u>去<u>金山寺</u>，要<u>法海和尚</u>放<u>許仙</u>回家。<u>法海和尚</u>見了<u>白娘子</u>，冷冷地說："白蛇精，你還來找我！趕快回你的<u>峨嵋山</u>去吧。要不然，我可不客氣了！"

<u>白娘子</u>見<u>法海和尚</u>就是不讓<u>許仙</u>回家，就拔下頭上的金釵，用手一劃，前面就出現了一條大河，往金山寺淹過去。<u>法海和尚</u>看見大水就要淹到金山寺了，趕快脫下₁₄他的袈裟₁₅，讓它變成一道長堤₁₆，把水攔₁₇在門外。<u>白娘子</u>的水高一尺，<u>法海</u>的堤就高一丈。就這樣，<u>白娘子</u>的水再大，也淹不到金山寺。因為<u>白娘子</u>懷孕了，身體不好，很快就被<u>法海</u>打敗了。打敗<u>白娘子</u>以後，<u>法海</u>把她壓在西湖邊的雷峰塔下，要她永遠見不到<u>許仙</u>，<u>許仙</u>也見不到她。可是，<u>小青</u>逃₁₈回了峨眉山，在那兒又修煉了十幾年，再回去找<u>法海和尚</u>。

找到<u>法海和尚</u>以後，<u>小青</u>跟他打了三天三夜，終於把他打敗了。然後<u>小青</u>救出了<u>許仙</u>和孩子，又一起去救<u>白娘子</u>。就這樣，<u>許仙</u>一家終於團圓了。從此，他們跟<u>小青</u>在一起，過著快樂的生活。

Vocabulary List

	SIMPLIFIED CHARACTERS	TRADITIONAL CHARACTERS	PINYIN	PART OF SPEECH	ENGLISH DEFINITION
1	白蛇	白蛇	bái shé	n.	white snake
	传	傳	zhuàn	n.	legend, story
2	蛇精	蛇精	shéjīng	n.	snake spirit
3	修炼	修煉	xiūliàn	v.	to practice asceticism
4	刮起	颳起	guāqǐ	vc.	to start blowing sharply (as a wind)
5	伞	傘	sǎn	n.	umbrella
6	遮雨	遮雨	zhēyǔ	vo.	to keep out the rain
7	淋湿	淋濕	línshī	v.	to drench
8	寺	寺	sì	n.	temple
9	烧香	燒香	shāo xiāng	vo.	to burn incense

	SIMPLIFIED CHARACTERS	TRADITIONAL CHARACTERS	PINYIN	PART OF SPEECH	ENGLISH DEFINITION
10	仙草	仙草	xiāncǎo	n.	celestial herbs
11	遇到	遇到	yùdào	vc.	to encounter
12	怀孕	懷孕	huáiyùn	v.	to be pregnant
13	关	關	guān	v.	to imprison
14	脱下	脫下	tuōxia	vc.	to take off
15	袈裟	袈裟	jiāshā	n.	*Kasaya* (vestment) for a Buddhist monk
16	堤	堤	dī	n.	embankment
17	拦	攔	lán	v.	to stop, to hinder, to block
18	逃	逃	táo	v.	to escape

Questions

1 Bai Suzhen and Xiao Qing were not ordinary people, but

    A. snakes under a curse who were banished from Emei Mountain.

    B. snake spirits from Emei Mountain who practiced asceticism for one thousand years.

    C. women from Emei Mountan who were under a curse that turned them into snakes.

    D. snake spirits from Emei Mountain who practiced asceticism for one hundred years.

2 How did Xu Xian first meet Bai Suzhen and Xiao Qing?

    A. He invited them to his home to avoid the rainstorm.

    B. He showed them around the West Lake on his boat.

    C. He held his umbrella for them to keep out of the rain.

    D. He asked to become their student.

3 Why was Monk Fahai angry with Bai Suzhen?

    A. Bai Suzhen began practicing medicine with Xu Xian.

    B. Many people went to Bai Suzhen when they were sick.

    C. Fewer people went to the temple to burn incense.

    D. All of the above.

4 What happened when Lady White Snake and Xu Xian drank the wine from Monk Fahai?

A. Xu Xian fell asleep and turned into a snake, scaring Lady White Snake to death.
B. Lady White Snake fell asleep and turned into a snake, scaring Xu Xian to death.
C. Both Xu Xian and Lady White Snake turned into snake spirits.
D. Both Xu Xian and Lady White Snake fell asleep.

5 Which of the following did not happen after Xu Xian was revived?

A. He was still afraid of snakes.
B. He still loved Lady White Snake even though she was a snake spirit.
C. He was convinced by Monk Fahai that she would eat him.
D. He and Lady White Snake learned they were going to be parents.

6 Monk Fahai prevented his temple from flooding by

A. creating an embankment with his clothing.
B. digging a trench around the temple.
C. absorbing the water with his clothing.
D. raising the temple higher and higher.

7 Who defeated Monk Fahai?

A. Xu Xian.

B. Lady White Snake.

C. Xiao Qing.

D. Lady White Snake and Xiao Qing.

DISCUSSION

1. From this story, what can you observe about the values of traditional Chinese society? Comparing Monk Fahai and Xu Xian's attitudes, how do you think spirits were viewed in ancient China?

2. This story existed as an oral legend long before it was written down, and has been adapted in operas, plays, films, and television series. One popular adaptation was a TV series called 《新白娘子传奇》 / 《新白娘子傳奇》. After researching online, explain what was unique about the show that made it so popular.

梁山伯與祝英台
梁山伯与祝英台

23

The Story of the Two Butterfly Lovers

梁山伯与祝英台
梁山伯與祝英台

Liáng Shānbó yǔ Zhù Yīngtái

很

久以前，有一位小姐，叫<u>祝英台</u>。<u>祝英台</u>长得很漂亮，也很聪明。她从小就喜欢读书，还会弹琴₁画画。因为那时候的女孩子不能上学，她只好每天坐在家里，看着男孩子去上学，心里羡慕₂极了！她对自己说："男孩子可以上学，我为什么不能呢？"

于是，她对爸爸妈妈说："我要跟哥哥们一样，到学校去学习。"爸爸说："不行！你是女孩子，怎么可以去上学呢？女孩子是不能走出家里的大门的！"<u>祝英台</u>想了一个办法。她让人去买了书生穿的衣服，回到房间，把衣服穿起来，去见爸爸妈妈。开始，她没说话，爸爸妈妈认不出她是谁，就问："请问这位书生，您找谁？"<u>祝英台</u>笑了，说："爸爸，妈妈，是我呀。我穿上男孩子的衣服，你们都认不出来，别人就更认不出我是女孩子了，你们就让我去上学吧！"

很久以前，有一位小姐，叫<u>祝英台</u>。<u>祝英台</u>長得很漂亮，也很聰明。她從小就喜歡讀書，還會彈琴₁畫畫。因為那時候的女孩子不能上學，她只好每天坐在家裡，看著男孩子去上學，心裡羨慕₂極了！她對自己說："男孩子可以上學，我為什麼不能呢？"

於是，她對爸爸媽媽說："我要跟哥哥們一樣，到學校去學習。"爸爸說："不行！你是女孩子，怎麼可以去上學呢？女孩子是不能走出家裡的大門的！"<u>祝英台</u>想了一個辦法。她讓人去買了書生穿的衣服，回到房間，把衣服穿起來，去見爸爸媽媽。開始，她沒說話，爸爸媽媽認不出她是誰，就問："請問這位書生，您找誰？"<u>祝英台</u>笑了，說："爸爸，媽媽，是我呀。我穿上男孩子的衣服，你們都認不出來，別人就更認不出我是女孩子了，你們就讓我去上學吧！"

第二天一早，祝英台就穿上了男孩子的衣服，高高兴兴地去上学了。路上，她遇到了梁山伯，他也是去上学的。他们就聊起天来，很快成了好朋友。到了学校，祝英台和梁山伯上课时，同坐一张桌子，下课以后又在一起看书学习，互相帮助。时间长了，祝英台觉得梁山伯越来越可爱。她想："要是能天天能跟他在一起，那多好啊！"梁山伯也很喜欢祝英台，觉得和她在一起很快乐，但是他不知道祝英台是个女孩子，只把她当做最好的朋友。三年很快过去了，学生们要毕业₃了。大家都很高兴，因为可以回家看爸爸妈妈了。可是，祝英台很难过，因为她已经爱上梁山伯了。回家的路上，他们俩一起走呀走呀，走了很久，就是不想分开₄。

突然，祝英台想到了一个办法，她对梁山伯说："我有一个小妹妹。她很聪明，也很漂亮，还没有结婚。过几天，你来我们家求婚₅吧。"梁山伯一听，高兴地说，"那太好了！我一定来！"

过了几天，梁山伯真的来了。他又惊又喜，因为他发现那个"小妹妹"不是别人，就是祝英台！可是，祝英台的爸爸妈妈不喜欢梁山伯，觉得他家里很穷。他们要女儿跟一个有钱人的儿子结婚。

第二天一早，祝英台就穿上了男孩子的衣服，高高興興地去上學了。路上，她遇到了梁山伯，他也是去上學的。他們就聊起天來，很快成了好朋友。到了學校，祝英台和梁山伯上課時，同坐一張桌子，下課以後又在一起看書學習，互相幫助。時間長了，祝英台覺得梁山伯越來越可愛。她想："要是能天天能跟他在一起，那多好啊！"梁山伯也很喜歡祝英台，覺得和她在一起很快樂，但是他不知道祝英台是個女孩子，只把她當做最好的朋友。三年很快過去了，學生們要畢業₃了。大家都很高興，因為可以回家看爸爸媽媽了。可是，祝英台很難過，因為她已經愛上梁山伯了。回家的路上，他們倆一起走呀走呀，走了很久，就是不想分開₄。

　　突然，祝英台想到了一個辦法，她對梁山伯說："我有一個小妹妹。她很聰明，也很漂亮，還沒有結婚。過幾天，你來我們家求婚₅吧。"梁山伯一聽，高興地說，"那太好了！我一定來！"

　　過了幾天，梁山伯真的來了。他又驚又喜，因為他發現那個"小妹妹"不是別人，就是祝英台！可是，祝英台的爸爸媽媽不喜歡梁山伯，覺得他家裡很窮。他們要女兒跟一個有錢人的兒子結婚。

梁山伯知道以后，心里很难过，很快就病倒了，没过多久就死了。梁山伯死了以后，祝英台穿上新娘子[6]的衣服，坐上了花轿[7]，去跟有钱人的儿子结婚。但是路上她一定要从梁山伯的墓[8]前经过[9]，跟他说再见。当轿子经过梁山伯墓前的时候，天突然变黑了。祝英台要花轿停下来，然后慢慢地走到梁山伯的墓前，一边哭，一边喊着他的名字。

就在这时候，天上刮起了大风，下起了大雨，雷电交加[10]，突然梁山伯的墓裂开了。祝英台好像听见梁山伯在里面喊她，她赶快跳进墓里。她一进去，墓就合上[11]了。慢慢地，风停了，雨也停了，一道彩虹[12]出现在天边，一对[13]美丽的蝴蝶[14]从墓里飞出来，它们快快乐乐地飞来飞去。这对蝴蝶就是梁山伯与祝英台。他们活着的时候不能在一起，死了以后变成蝴蝶，从此永远不分开。

梁山伯知道以後，心裡很難過，很快就病倒了，沒過多久就死了。梁山伯死了以後，祝英台穿上新娘子[6]的衣服，坐上了花轎[7]，去跟有錢人的兒子結婚。但是路上她一定要從梁山伯的墓[8]前經過[9]，跟他說再見。當轎子經過梁山伯墓前的時候，天突然變黑了。祝英台要花轎停下來，然後慢慢地走到梁山伯的墓前，一邊哭，一邊喊著他的名字。

就在這時候，天上刮起了大風，下起了大雨，雷電交加[10]，突然梁山伯的墓裂開了。祝英台好像聽見梁山伯在裡面喊她，她趕快跳進墓裡。她一進去，墓就合上[11]了。慢慢地，風停了，雨也停了，一道彩虹[12]出現在天邊，一對[13]美麗的蝴蝶[14]從墓裡飛出來，它們快快樂樂地飛來飛去。這對蝴蝶就是梁山伯與祝英台。他們活著的時候不能在一起，死了以後變成蝴蝶，從此永遠不分開。

他們變成蝴蝶，從此永遠不分開

Vocabulary List

	SIMPLIFIED CHARACTERS	TRADITIONAL CHARACTERS	PINYIN	PART OF SPEECH	ENGLISH DEFINITION
1	弹琴	彈琴	tán qín	vo.	to play a stringed musical instrument
2	羡慕	羨慕	xiànmù	v.	to envy
3	毕业	畢業	bìyè	v.	to graduate
4	分开	分開	fēnkāi	vc.	to separate, to be separated
5	求婚	求婚	qiúhūn	vo.	to propose marriage
6	新娘子	新娘子	xīnniángzi	n.	bride
7	花轿	花轎	huājiào	n.	bridal sedan
8	墓	墓	mù	n.	grave
9	经过	經過	jīngguò	v.	to pass by
10	雷电交加	雷電交加	léidiàn jiāojiā	ce.	thunder and lightning
11	合上	合上	héshang	vc.	to (be) shut
12	彩虹	彩虹	cǎihóng	n.	rainbow
13	对	對	duì	mw.	pair
14	蝴蝶	蝴蝶	húdié	n.	butterfly

the story of the two butterfly lovers　梁山伯与祝英台

Questions

Why did Zhu Yingtai dress up like a boy?

A. She wanted her parents to pay more attention to her.

B. She wanted to play games with the boys.

C. She wanted to go to school.

D. She wanted to get closer with Liang Shanbo.

When Zhu Yingtai dressed up like a boy and showed her parents, they

A. were overjoyed and allowed her to go to school.

B. did not recognize her.

C. became angry and did not allow her to go to school.

D. recognized her right away.

As classmates, Zhu Yingtai and Liang Shanbo

A. studied together and grew fond of each other.

B. competed with each other and became rivals.

C. studied together but did not become close friends.

D. competed with each other but became close friends.

How did Zhu Yingtai convince Liang Shanbo to visit her at her house?

A. She revealed her true identity.

B. She told him that she had a sister.

C. She told him that she had a secret.

D. She told him that her parents wanted him to marry her.

5 Why was Liang Shanbo sad when he visited Zhu Yingtai's home?

A. He realized that Zhu Yingtai did not have a sister.

B. He realized that Zhu Yingtai's parents wanted him to marry her sister.

C. He realized that Zhu Yingtai was a girl all along.

D. He realized that Zhu Yingtai's parents did not want her to marry him.

6 What happened when Zhu Yingtai visited Liang Shanbo's grave?

A. Liang Shanbo turned into a butterfly and followed Zhu Yingtai to her wedding.

B. Liang Shanbo's grave split open and Zhu Yingtai fell to her death.

C. Liang Shanbo's grave split open and Zhu Yingtai jumped inside.

D. Zhu Yingtai died from a broken heart and was buried next to Liang Shanbo.

7 Which of the following did not happen after Zhu Yingtai visited Liang Shanbo's grave?

A. The rain and wind stopped.

B. A rainbow appeared in the sky.

C. Liang Shanbo emerged from the clouds.

D. A pair of butterflies emerged from the grave.

DISCUSSION	2. Have you ever heard the story of Hua Mulan? What similar challenges did Hua Mulan and Zhu Yingtai encounter that made them decide to dress up like boys?
1. Why do you think the two lovers are represented as butterflies?	3. What are some famous love stories in your culture? How are they similar to or different from the story about Liang Shanbo and Zhu Yingtai?

牛郎織女的故事

牛郎织女的故事

24

The Story of Cowherd and Weaving Girl

牛郎织女₁的故事
牛郎織女₁的故事

Niú láng Zhī nǚ de gù shi

很久很久以前，有一个孩子叫<u>牛郎</u>。他很小的时候，爸爸妈妈就死了，家里只有一头₂老牛。他每天晚上没地方睡觉，只好跟老牛睡在一起，所以大家都叫他<u>牛郎</u>。

<u>牛郎</u>是个好孩子，他很友好₃，也很勤劳。他每天一早就牵着老牛到地里去工作，晚上很晚才回家，生活过得很辛苦。这时候，天上有一位织布₄的仙女，叫<u>织女</u>。<u>织女</u>每天都得为天上的<u>王母娘娘</u>织布。有一天，<u>织女</u>织布织累了，她停下来往下面看了看，正好看见<u>牛郎</u>在地里工作。<u>织女</u>觉得<u>牛郎</u>又好看又勤劳，就每天都从天上看着他，很快就爱上他了。<u>织女</u>看见<u>牛郎</u>每天回家以后，还要自己做饭洗衣服，晚上又跟老牛睡在一起，就很想帮助他。所以，她决定从天上下来，去找<u>牛郎</u>。

很久很久以前，有一個孩子叫牛郎。他很小的時候，爸爸媽媽就死了，家裡只有一頭₂老牛。他每天晚上沒地方睡覺，只好跟老牛睡在一起，所以大家都叫他牛郎。

牛郎是個好孩子，他很友好₃，也很勤勞。他每天一早就牽著老牛到地裡去工作，晚上很晚才回家，生活過得很辛苦。這時候，天上有一位織布₄的仙女，叫織女。織女每天都得為天上的王母娘娘織布。有一天，織女織布織累了，她停下來往下面看了看，正好看見牛郎在地裡工作。織女覺得牛郎又好看又勤勞，就每天都從天上看著他，很快就愛上他了。織女看見牛郎每天回家以后，還要自己做飯洗衣服，晚上又跟老牛睡在一起，就很想幫助他。所以，她決定從天上下來，去找牛郎。

有一天，<u>牛郎</u>在地里工作完了，牵着老牛回家，突然看见一位美丽的姑娘站在他面前，他太高兴了。<u>织女</u>告诉<u>牛郎</u>，她很想帮助他，跟他一起生活，让他过得快快乐乐。<u>牛郎</u>听了，很高兴地说："那你做我的妻子吧。"<u>织女</u>的脸红$_5$了。她点了点头，同意了。<u>牛郎</u>和<u>织女</u>很快就结婚了。结婚以后，老牛还跟他们住在一起。每天，<u>牛郎</u>去地里工作，<u>织女</u>在家里织布，他们生活得很快乐。又过了几年，<u>牛郎</u>和<u>织女</u>生了一个男孩子，和一个女孩子，一家人过得更快乐了。

可是，有一天，天上突然雷电交加，<u>织女</u>一下子不见了。两个孩子看不见妈妈，大哭起来。<u>牛郎</u>也着急了。可是过了一会儿，天气又好了，<u>织女</u>也回家了，但她的脸上却满是泪水$_6$。她抱$_7$着孩子，又拉$_8$着<u>牛郎</u>，一边哭一边说："我是天上王母娘娘的<u>织女</u>，现在，他们要我回去…"话还没说完，几个天兵天将$_9$就到了他们家门口，把<u>织女</u>带走了。

<u>牛郎</u>抱着两个孩子，很着急，说："不行，我不能让妻子就这样走了，我不能让孩子没有母亲，我要去找她，我一定要把她找回来！"

有一天，牛郎在地裡工作完了，牽著老牛回家，突然看見一位美麗的姑娘站在他面前，他太高興了。織女告訴牛郎，她很想幫助他，跟他一起生活，讓他過得快快樂樂。牛郎聽了，很高興地說："那你做我的妻子吧。"織女的臉紅5了。她點了點頭，同意了。牛郎和織女很快就結婚了。結婚以后，老牛還跟他們住在一起。每天，牛郎去地裡工作，織女在家裡織布，他們生活得很快樂。又過了幾年，牛郎和織女生了一個男孩子，和一個女孩子，一家人過得更快樂了。

可是，有一天，天上突然雷電交加，織女一下子不見了。兩個孩子看不見媽媽，大哭起來。牛郎也著急了。可是過了一會兒，天氣又好了，織女也回家了，但她的臉上卻滿是淚水6。她抱7著孩子，又拉8著牛郎，一邊哭一邊說："我是天上王母娘娘的織女，現在，他們要我回去…"話還沒說完，幾個天兵天將9就到了他們家門口，把織女帶走了。

牛郎抱著兩個孩子，很著急，說："不行，我不能讓妻子就這樣走了，我不能讓孩子沒有母親，我要去找她，我一定要把她找回來！"

把织女带走

这时候，那头老牛突然说话了，它对牛郎说："别难过！你抱着两个孩子，快骑₁₀到我背上来。"牛郎听见老牛说话，觉得很奇怪，但还是抱着孩子，骑上了老牛的背，没想到老牛一下子就飞了起来，一直飞到了天上。

可是，到了天上，王母娘娘不想让织女看见牛郎和孩子，她想出了一个办法。

她找来七个蒙着脸₁₁、长得一样高的姑娘，对牛郎说："你认吧，认出了谁是你的妻子，你就带她回家。"牛郎一看，七个姑娘都是一样的，他认不出哪一个是织女。但是他的两个孩子却叫着"妈妈"，飞快地向一个姑娘跑去，一下子就把织女找出来了。

老牛一下就飛了起來

這時候，那頭老牛突然說話了，它對牛郎說："別難過！你抱著兩個孩子，快騎[10]到我背上來。"牛郎聽見老牛說話，覺得很奇怪，但還是抱著孩子，騎上了老牛的背，沒想到老牛一下子就飛了起來，一直飛到了天上。

可是，到了天上，王母娘娘不想讓織女看見牛郎和孩子，她想出了一個辦法。

她找來七個蒙著臉[11]、長得一樣高的姑娘，對牛郎說："你認吧，認出了誰是你的妻子，你就帶她回家。"牛郎一看，七個姑娘都是一樣的，他認不出哪一個是織女。但是他的兩個孩子卻叫著"媽媽"，王母娘娘没办法，但她还是不想让织女跟牛郎一起回去，就叫天兵天将把织女带走了。牛郎一看，着急了，牵着两个孩子追上去。牛郎和孩子跑呀跑呀，跑累了也不停下来，马上就要追上织女了。王母娘娘一看，着急了。她拔下[12]头上的金簪[13]，用手一划[14]，牛郎和织女中间就出现了一条大河，这就是我们的银河[15]。

这条银河又宽[16]又长，连老牛也飞不过去。牛郎和织女只能站在银河的两边，互相望[17]着，一边哭，一边叫着对方[18]的名字。他们就这样每天望着，哭着，最后感动了天上的喜鹊[19]。喜鹊们在一起开了个会，决定帮助牛郎和织女，用自己的身体在河上架[20]起一座桥[21]，让牛郎织女一家在桥上团聚[22]。这一天是七月七日。

从那以后，每年到了七月七日，成千上万[23]的喜鹊就会飞过来，聚在一起，在银河上架起一座长长的鹊桥，让牛郎织女一家在桥上团聚。为了庆祝牛郎织女每年一次的团聚，中国人决定把七月七日作为中国的情人节[24]。

飛快地向一個姑娘跑去，一下子就把織女找出來了。

　　王母娘娘沒辦法，但她還是不想讓織女跟牛郎一起回去，就叫天兵天將把織女帶走了。牛郎一看，著急了，牽著兩個孩子追上去。牛郎和孩子跑呀跑呀，跑累了也不停下來，馬上就要追上織女了。王母娘娘一看，著急了。她拔下[12]頭上的金簪[13]，用手一劃[14]，牛郎和織女中間就出現了一條大河，這就是我們的銀河[15]。

　　這條銀河又寬[16]又長，連老牛也飛不過去。牛郎和織女只能站在銀河的兩邊，互相望[17]著，一邊哭，一邊叫著對方[18]的名字。他們就這樣每天望著，哭著，最后感動了天上的喜鵲[19]。喜鵲們在一起開了個會，決定幫助牛郎和織女，用自己的身體在河上架[20]起一座橋[21]，讓牛郎織女一家在橋上團聚[22]。這一天是七月七日。

　　從那以后，每年到了七月七日，成千上萬[23]的喜鵲就會飛過來，聚在一起，在銀河上架起一座長長的鵲橋，讓牛郎織女一家在橋上團聚。為了慶祝牛郎織女每年一次的團聚，中國人決定把七月七日作為中國的情人節[24]。

Vocabulary List

	SIMPLIFIED CHARACTERS	TRADITIONAL CHARACTERS	PINYIN	PART OF SPEECH	ENGLISH DEFINITION
1	牛郎	牛郎	Niúláng	pn.	Cowherd
	织女	織女	Zhīnǚ	pn.	Weaving Girl
2	头	頭	tóu	mw.	(measure word for big animals)
3	友好	友好	yǒuhǎo	adj.	friendly
4	织布	織布	zhībù	vo.	to weave cloth
5	脸红	臉紅	liǎnhóng	vc.	to blush
6	泪水	淚水	lèishuǐ	n.	tears
7	抱	抱	bào	v.	to hold
8	拉	拉	lā	v.	to pull
9	天兵天将	天兵天將	tiānbīng tiānjiàng	n.	heavenly warriors
10	骑	騎	qí	v.	to mount
11	蒙着脸	蒙著臉	méngzhe liǎn	vo.	to be masked
12	拔下	拔下	báxià	v.	to take off

	SIMPLIFIED CHARACTERS	TRADITIONAL CHARACTERS	PINYIN	PART OF SPEECH	ENGLISH DEFINITION
13	金簪	金簪	jīnzān	n.	gold hairpin
14	划	劃	huà	v.	to slash
15	银河	銀河	Yínhé	pn.	Milky Way
16	宽	寬	kuān	adj.	wide
17	望	望	wàng	v.	to stare at
18	对方	對方	duìfāng	n.	the other party
19	喜鹊	喜鵲	xǐquè	n.	magpie
20	架	架	jià	v.	to build
21	桥	橋	qiáo	n.	bridge
22	团聚	團聚	tuánjù	v.	to be reunited
23	成千上万	成千上萬	chéng qiān shàng wàn	ce.	tens of thousands
24	情人节	情人節	Qíngrénjié	pn.	Valentine's Day

1 One day, when Weaving Girl was tired of weaving, she looked down from the heavens and saw that

    A. Cowherd was asleep in the fields with his cow.

    B. Cowherd was still working hard in the fields.

    C. the cow was grazing on the cloth that she was weaving.

    D. Cowherd was helping her weave the cloth from down below.

2 Weaving Girl wanted to help Cowherd because

    A. after a day of hard work, he still had to cook and clean by himself.

    B. he needed someone to help him work in the fields.

    C. after a day of hard work, he still had to help Weaving Girl with her cloth.

    D. he needed someone to help him take care of his cow.

3 Which of these did not happen when Weaving Girl was taken away by the heavenly warriors?

    A. The cow began to speak.

    B. Cowherd left his children behind to save Weaving Girl.

    C. The cow flew into the heavens.

    D. Cowherd and his children rode on the cow's back.

4 What was the Heavenly Queen's plan to keep Cowherd and Weaving Girl apart?

A. She tempted Cowherd by allowing him to choose one of her seven daughters to marry.

B. She had Cowherd's children try to recognize their mother among seven identical women.

C. She tempted Cowherd by allowing him to marry all of her seven daughters.

D. She had Cowherd try to recognize his wife among seven identical women.

5 How did the Heavenly Queen's plan fail?

A. Cowherd and his cow recognized Weaving Girl right away.

B. The seven women were not all the same height.

C. Weaving Girl's children recognized their mother right away.

D. The seven women did not all have masks.

6 What did the Heavenly Queen do after her first plan failed?

A. She turned her gold hairpin into a river, which became known as the Milky Way.

B. She used her gold hairpin to defeat Cowherd and his cow.

C. She gave her gold hairpin to the heavenly warriors to defeat Cowherd and his cow.

D. She gave up and allowed Cowherd and Weaving Girl to be together.

7 How did the flock of magpies help Cowherd and Weaving Girl?

A. Cowherd rode on the backs of the magpies to cross the Milky Way and reunite with Weaving Girl.

B. The magpies formed a bridge on which Cowherd and Weaving Girl could reunite once a year.

C. Weaving Girl rode on the backs of the magpies to cross the Milky Way and reunite with Cowherd.

D. The magpies formed a bridge on which Cowherd and Weaving Girl could reunite every day.

DISCUSSION

1. What is the origin of Valentine's Day in the West? Compared to the Chinese Valentine's Day, which do you think is more interesting or romantic, and why?

2. What does this story share in common with other stories such as "Beauty in the Painting" and "The Love Story of a Fish Spirit"? How do these similarities reflect traditional Chinese gender roles? Are they similar to traditional gender roles in your culture?

APPENDIX:
STORY ABSTRACTS IN ENGLISH

I: FABLES AND LITERARY ADAPTATIONS

1. ## THE MAN FROM THE STATE OF ZHENG WHO NEEDED NEW SHOES

Once upon a time, there was a gentleman from the State of Zheng. He lived far from the nearest market, which only opened every once in a while. So each time before he went to market, he took pains to make a shopping list, just in case he might forget what he needed. One day, he noticed his shoes were completely worn out. He decided to buy a new pair when the market opened. He carefully measured his feet with a string and wrote down their size. When the day finally came, he rushed to the market and found a pair of shoes he liked. However, he forgot to bring the string with him! So he rushed back home, got the string, and ran back to the market. However, by the time he reached the market, he was disappointed to find that the shoe stall was already closed.

2. ## SUSPECTING HIS NEIGHBOR OF STEALING AN AX

A long time ago, there was a poor man who made a living by selling kindling wood. One day, he went to the mountains to collect wood, but upon returning home, he could not find his ax anywhere. He looked around his house with no success. Just then, he saw his neighbor pass by. For some reason, he felt his neighbor was acting nervous, and suspected that his neighbor had stolen his ax. Then he started to observe his neighbor, and the more he observed, the more his neighbor looked like a thief to him. Having no evidence with which to confront his neighbor, however, the man had to buy a new ax and went back to the mountains to collect wood a few days later. While on his way, he saw his lost ax. He had dropped it the last time he was carrying his bundles of wood home. From then on, his neighbor no longer seemed like someone who would steal an ax.

3. ## THE MAN FROM THE STATE OF QI WHO FEARED THE SKY WOULD FALL

In ancient China, there was a man living in the State of Qi. He was always worried that something unfortunate might happen. What worried him most was that the sky might fall, and what made his fear even worse was that he didn't know when it would fall and, if it did, where he could hide. He was so worried that he could not eat or sleep. When his friends heard about his fears, they thought he was absurd. They told him that the sky was so high and far away that it would never fall, and that worrying about it every day would not help him one bit. Still, the man couldn't help but preoccupy himself with incessant worries and fears, and he soon fell ill and died.

4. ## THERE IS NO SILVER BURIED HERE!

Once upon a time, there were two next-door neighbors who lived near a marketplace. One of them was called Zhang San (张三 / 張三), and the other was Wang Er (王二). Zhang San worked very hard at peddling wares in the market. His greatest wish was to save up 300 ounces of silver and then retire. Finally, to his delight, he saved up those 300 ounces of silver, but started to worry about where to hide it. There were no banks in China at the time, and 300 ounces of silver was too heavy a load to carry around. So, he decided to bury it underground. One night, he dug a hole in his yard and buried the silver there. But he soon worried that somebody might steal it, so he put up a note beside the buried treasure that read: "There is not 300 ounces of silver buried here." However, his neighbor, Wang Er, was watching him all this time. He excavated the silver and put up another note that read: "Your neighbor, Wang Er, did not steal your silver!"

5. YE GONG LOVES DRAGONS

There once was a man by the name of Ye Gong (叶公 / 葉公) who liked dragons very much. He had depictions of dragons all over his house, including the walls, rooftop, pillars, doors, windows, and furniture, and even on his clothes. In addition, he liked to draw dragons and had a talent for it. The dragons he drew looked very real. He often let people know that his biggest wish was to see a real dragon, face to face. The Sky Dragon was delighted to hear about this and decided to make Ye Gong's wish come true. One night, the Sky Dragon arrived at Ye Gong's house and saw him asleep. Awakened by the thunder and lightning brought by the Sky Dragon, Ye Gong was frightened half to death when he saw a real dragon in his house. He immediately ran for his life and never mentioned another dragon again.

6. YU GONG REMOVES THE MOUNTAINS

Once upon a time, there was a small, remote village deep in the mountains. The villagers could not find an easy outlet to the outside world, and had to climb up and down the mountains. In the village lived two old men. One of them was stubborn and determined, so he was called Yu Gong (愚公, Stubborn Old Man). The other considered himself to be very smart, and was called Zhi Sou (智叟, Smart Old Man). All his life, Yu Gong had experienced the inconvenience and difficulty caused by the big mountains and he did not want his fellow villagers and descendants to experience the same difficulties. So, he decided to remove the mountains. He gathered his family and started to dig out the mountains bit by bit. Soon the other villagers joined him. Zhi Sou found this absurd. However, the Heavenly God was touched by Yu Gong's determination and sent his heavenly soldiers to remove the mountains once and for all.

7. FOX PUTS ON TIGER'S POWER

Amongst a kingdom of animals in a big forest, the tiger was king because he was the strongest. The tiger was so powerful and so threatening that the animals fled for their lives whenever they spotted him. He fully enjoyed this status, and often strutted around the forest to show off. One day, a fox inadvertently bumped into him. The offended tiger grabbed the poor fox and was about to eat him up. When the fox saw no way to escape, an idea flashed into his mind. He said to the tiger, "I was just appointed by the Heavenly Emperor to be the new king of this forest. Dare you eat me?" The tiger was stunned and confused, but he did not believe the fox. So the fox invited the tiger to walk around the forest with him. To the tiger's great surprise, he saw all the animals immediately fleeing for their lives when they saw the two of them. He never realized that it was he himself who caused them to flee.

8. AIMING FOR THE SOUTH BUT HEADING FOR THE NORTH

Ancient China was divided into many small states. One of them was the state of Chu, located in the south, and another was the state of Wei, located in the north. A man from Wei set off on a business trip to the state of Chu, but he was headed north instead of south. Because he believed that he had the fastest horse and had hired the most skillful horseman, and brought with him a large quantity of money, he was certain that he would reach his destination. On his way north, he bumped into a friend who told him that he was going in the wrong direction. The man from Wei paid no attention to his friend's advice and believed that he would have no problem reaching the state of Chu. He then continued moving farther and farther away from his intended destination.

9. BO LE DISCOVERS THE BEST HORSE

In ancient China, horses played a very important role in people's lives. People relied on horses for travel, to fight battles, and to pull carts. Thus everybody desired a good horse, especially a "one-thousand-*li* horse," which was said to be able to run one thousand *li* (500 meters) per day. But such horses were hard to find. There was a man by the name of Bo Le (伯乐 / 伯樂), who was said to have the ability to discern good horses from weak ones. One day, he saw a horse laboriously pulling a heavy cart. The poor horse looked old and skinny, and was about to collapse. Bo Le knew immediately that this horse was one of the best, so he fed the horse with his own food and dressed it with his own clothes. The horse seemed to appreciate his kindness very much. He leaned against Bo Le's chest and gave a loud cry that seemed to say, "thank you." Bo Le bought the horse for himself and took great care of it. Soon the horse grew big and strong, and became a famous "one-thousand-*li* horse."

10. LEARNING TO WALK IN HANDAN

In ancient China, there was a famous city by the name of Handan, whose citizens had unique and graceful postures. When they walked, their pace was brisk and beautiful. People from all over swarmed into the city to learn how the people of Handan walked. Among the swarms was a man from the state of Yan. He felt that the walking style of his fellow countrymen was ugly, so he went to Handan and watched people walk on the street every day. Soon, he started to imitate the Handan style. However, to his great disappointment, he could not walk like the Handan people no matter how hard he tried. He soon ran out of money and had to quit, but by then he had forgotten how to walk. In the end, he had to crawl back home!

II: TALES OF TRADITIONAL FESTIVALS

11. TALES OF THE CHINESE NEW YEAR

The first day of the lunar year is the most important festival in China, and is called *Chunjie* (春节 / 春節, Spring Festival) or *guonian* (过年 / 過年, celebrating the New Year). Chinese people start the New Year celebration half a month before and continue for half a month after this day, which means there is a full month of festivities and excitement. The grand celebration takes place on New Year's Eve, during which time families reunite and share delicious dishes and refreshments. They also hang red banners on their doors, set off deafening fireworks, and play games all night long. On New Year's Day, everybody wears new clothes and visits one another's homes to *bainian* (拜年, to wish one another a happy new year). To children's great delight, they get presents—mostly pocket money wrapped up in red envelopes called *hongbao* (红包 / 紅包).

Why do Chinese people speak of celebrating New Year's as *guonian*? Of course, there is a story behind this. There was a vicious monster by the name of Nian (年, year), who lived in the mountains but came to the village to wreak all kinds of havoc on New Year's Eve. To scare the monster away, people put up red banners and set off loud fireworks. On New Year's Day, they celebrated their victory over the monster, and called it *guonian*.

12. TALES OF THE LANTERN FESTIVAL

The grand lunar Chinese New Year celebration ends with another important Chinese festival, called *Yuanxiaojie* (元宵节 / 元宵節), on the 15th day of the first month of the new year. Chinese people celebrate this festival with big feasts, thunderous fireworks, and glowing red lanterns. The Lantern Festival is associated with another story of wisdom and victory.

Once upon a time, a hunter accidentally shot down a celestial bird, which greatly angered the Heavenly God, who decided to punish all humans. He ordered his celestial soldiers to set the earth on fire and burn down everybody and everything. Having overheard this plan, the Heavenly Daughter was very upset. To help the humans, she sent them a secret message and warned them about the coming calamity. At first, people were in a great panic, but they soon came up with a plan. They lit up a sea of red lanterns and set off thunderous fireworks, and the Heavenly God was satisfied when he saw the earth from afar engulfed in a "sea of fire." To celebrate their victory, Chinese people proclaimed this day as another festival, and have celebrated with fireworks and red lanterns ever since.

13. THE DRAGON BOAT FESTIVAL AND THE POET QU YUAN

The Dragon Boat Festival is another traditional Chinese festival, occurring on the fifth day of the fifth month in the Chinese lunar calendar. The Dragon Boat Festival is marked by unique rituals such as boat races and throwing glutinous rice wrapped in bamboo leaves into the river, both of which are meant to commemorate a famous poet by the name of Qu Yuan (屈原).

In Qu Yuan's time, China was divided into many small hostile states, including the major states of Chu and Qin. Qu Yuan was a high-ranking official of Chu, and he loved his state passionately. Seeing the threat from the state of Qin, Qu Yuan worried about his people, and made many suggestions to the King of Chu in order to strengthen the state. However, the king turned a deaf ear to Qu Yuan, discharged him, and sent him into exile. While in exile, Qu Yuan wrote many beautiful poems in praise of his people. One day, he heard that his state of Chu had been invaded and that the king had been taken as a prisoner of war. Heartbroken, Qu Yuan jumped into the river and drowned himself. This day happened to be the fifth day of the fifth month. With great admiration, Chinese people have since dedicated this day to Qu Yuan and celebrate it in his memory.

14. TALES OF THE MID-AUTUMN FESTIVAL

The Mid-Autumn Festival (中秋节 / 中秋節) is the fourth and last important festival of the Chinese lunar year. This is a festival of family reunion and a grand celebration of the agricultural harvest. To celebrate, people eat moon cakes and freshly harvested produce. By tradition, people sit in the moonlight that evening, enjoying the festive food, the bright moon, and their families' company. Like all other traditional Chinese festivals, there is a touching story behind the Mid-Autumn Festival.

Once upon a time, there were ten burning suns in the sky, which dried up the land and threatened people's lives. To help people overcome this calamity, a hero by the name of Houyi (后羿) shot down nine of the suns and kept just one in the sky. Houyi had a beautiful wife by the name of Chang E (嫦娥). He obtained some celestial elixir to share with her, so that they could become immortal and live happily ever after. However, Chang E ate it all by accident! The elixir's magical power sent her floating up to the moon, where she has been ever since. As a result, this beloved husband and wife were separated, with one left on the earth and the other living on the lonely moon. This story thus adds an emotional sentiment to the Mid-Autumn Festival: we should always keep close ties to our families, and enjoy one another while we can.

15. CANG JIE INVENTS THE CHINESE WRITING SCRIPT

Long ago in China, there was no writing script or characters. In order to record information, people tied strings into knots. For instance, someone who had 100 fish would tie 100 knots, which was very cumbersome and inefficient. Then a smart man by the name of Cang Jie (仓颉 / 倉頡) decided to invent a better way. He tried many different ways, with no initial success. Then one day, he saw a strange footprint in the ground and went to ask a hunter what it was. The hunter told him that it was the footprint of a chicken. It dawned on him that everything in the world could be represented by its own distinctive feature. He then started to observe his surroundings and created all kinds of symbols, which became the origins of today's Chinese pictographic script.

16. THE GOD OF MATCHMAKING

How does a man meet a woman, fall in love with her, and then marry her? Chinese people believe that such events are prearranged by the God of Matchmaking. As one legend goes, a young man by the name of Wei Gu (韦固 / 韋固) saw an old man reading a gigantic book in the moonlight. Curious, Wei Gu went over and asked what he was reading. The old man told Wei Gu that his book kept the record of all marriages in the world, and that he matched up each couple with a tiny red thread—no matter how far away they were from one other. The old man checked his book and found Wei Gu's future wife: a poor, five-year-old girl bearing a scar between her brows. Wei Gu found the prediction ridiculous and quickly forgot about it. Many years later, however, he got married and found that his beautiful bride was the very girl from the old man's prediction.

17. THE STORY OF THE TWELVE ZODIAC ANIMALS

In the Chinese tradition, the twelve-year zodiac cycle is represented by twelve animals: the rat, cow, tiger, rabbit, dragon, snake, horse, sheep, monkey, chicken, dog, and pig. At the very beginning, the Jade Emperor selected these animals to represent each year, but had a hard time deciding who should come first, and who should follow. To solve this problem, he invited the animals to participate in a competition to earn their own place in the zodiac. Interestingly, the tiny rat won first place, ahead of all of the contestants. How could such a thing have happened? If you pay close attention to the rat's clever trick, you will see for yourself!

18. DRAGON EYES

A long time ago, there was a very famous artist by the name of Zhang Sengyao (张僧繇 / 張僧繇). His paintings were very realistic. Although many people desired his artwork, he very rarely painted for others. One day, he visited a temple, where the monk enthusiastically entertained him. After serving Zhang with his best refreshments, the monk requested that Zhang paint a dragon on the wall of the front hall. Feeling obligated, Zhang painted one, but omitted its eyes. The monk wondered why, and insisted that the dragon should have eyes. Zhang said that if he filled them in, the dragon might become real. The monk did not believe him and accused Zhang of cheating him. With no choice, Zhang started to fill in the dragon's eyes. But before he could even put down his brush, there was a huge bang. All of a sudden, the dragon came alive and flew away, leaving the monk with nothing but a large hole in his wall.

19. LITTLE NEZHA FIGHTS THE GREAT DRAGON KING

Once upon a time, there was a General by the name of Li Jing (李靖). His wife had been pregnant for three years, and was finally approaching labor. Li Jing rushed to see his newborn, but what he saw instead was a big, red ball of flesh rolling around. He slashed the ball open with his sword. All of a sudden, a glowing light filled the room, and there lay a smiling little boy. Thinking that the incident was most inauspicious, Li Jing had decided to kill the baby, when an immortal by the name of Taiyi Zhenren (太乙真人) appeared. He told Li Jing that his baby would be a great hero, and gave the baby three magical items: a pair of wind-fire wheels, a universe ring (a type of weapon), and a red silk sash.

The baby's life was thus spared, and he was named Nezha (哪吒). One day, when Nezha was seven years old, he went to bathe in the East Sea. As he was splashing around happily, his red silk sash—a manifestation of fire—caused the sea to boil and shook the Dragon King's palace at the bottom of the ocean. The Dragon King was furious and came to attack the troublemaker, only to get seriously injured by Nezha. The Dragon King was enraged and swiftly flooded Nezha's home city. Nezha pleaded for the Dragon King to spare his people, saying that he would pay for the Dragon King's anger with his own life. There and then, Nezha committed suicide. At the moment of Nezha's death, Taiyi Zhenren arrived. He reincarnated Nezha and taught him even more magical skills, and Nezha became a great hero of his people. He rode on his wind-fire wheels and traveled everywhere, fighting evil.

The legend of Nezha is extremely popular throughout China. Today, Nezha's birthday is celebrated with much gusto on the eighth and ninth days of the fourth month of the Chinese calendar.

IV: CLASSIC TALES OF LOVE AND ROMANCE

20. BEAUTY IN THE PAINTING

Once upon a time, there was a poor young student who had no family and no possessions except for a painting of a beautiful girl. He worked very hard to make ends meet. Every morning before he left for work, he would look at the girl in the painting and say good-bye to her. One day, when he returned home, he found his house thoroughly cleaned, his clothes washed, and a hot meal on the table. The same thing happened for several consecutive days. Finally, one day he waited outside to catch sight of who was taking care of these things, and he saw that it was the girl in the painting who had cooked and cleaned for him. The girl had been a fairy in heaven but was put under a curse by the Heavenly Queen, by which she was frozen in the painting. The young man's affection for the girl had gradually removed the curse and freed her so that she could walk out of the painting and live happily ever after with him.

21. THE LOVE STORY OF A FISH SPIRIT

Once upon a time, there was a wealthy man whose name was Jin Chong (金宠 / 金寵). He had a beautiful daughter called Lady Mudan (牡丹), meaning "peony." Meanwhile, Jin Chong's old friend had a son named Zhang Zhen (张珍 / 張珍), whose given name means "treasure." Jin Chong and his friend were fond of each other's children and arranged for them to be married. Unfortunately, Zhang Zhen's parents both died soon after, and he lost everything. Jin Chong's family thus became very cold toward him. They placed him in a shabby straw shed near their family pond. Sad and lonely, Zhang Zhen talked to a beautiful carp in the pond every day. He was unaware that the carp was not a regular fish, but actually a spirit. The fish spirit fell in love with Zhang Zhen and transformed herself into the likeness of the beautiful Lady Mudan. Every day, she came to see him and took good care of him. Zhang Zhen believed she was the true Lady Mudan. Three years later, Zhang Zhen passed the Imperial Examination and was awarded a high-ranking position. The two Lady Mudans had a bitter fight with each other, for both claimed love for Zhang Zhen and wanted to marry him. With the help of the Bodhisattva Guanyin, he finally found his true love.

22. LADY WHITE SNAKE

Once upon a time, two snake spirits—one white and one green—transformed themselves into female human forms after thousands of years of self-cultivation on Emei Mountain. They called themselves Bai Suzhen (白素贞 / 白素貞) and Xiao Qing (小青). One day, at the scenic West Lake in Hangzhou, they came across a young man called Xu Xian (许仙 / 許仙). Bai and Xu fell in love at first sight. After they got married, the couple practiced medicine, and they lived a happy life. However, their practices offended Monk Fahai (法海和尚) of the Jinshan Temple, who kidnapped Xu and overpowered Bai. Then he imprisoned Bai in the gigantic Leifeng Pagoda. The Green Snake (小青), who had escaped from the monk, went back to Mount Emei for further self-cultivation. Years later, she returned to free Bai and Xu. With her new magic powers, she defeated the Monk Fahai. Xu and his family were thus rescued and reunited.

23. THE STORY OF TWO BUTTERFLY LOVERS

Once upon a time, a beautiful young lady named Zhu Yingtai (祝英台) disguised herself as a boy traveling to study far away from home. During her journey, she met Liang Shanbo (梁山伯), a fellow schoolmate. They studied together for three years and became very fond of each other. When they parted, Yingtai offered to arrange for Shanbo to marry her younger sister. After arriving at Yingtai's home, Shanbo was overjoyed to find out that her "younger sister" was in fact Yingtai herself. Although they were deeply in love with each other, Yingtai's parents arranged for her to marry a rich man instead. Heartbroken, Shanbo became very ill and died soon after. On her way to be married, Yingtai insisted on passing by Shanbo's grave to pay her last respects for him. Amidst fierce lightning and thunder, Shanbo's grave split open, and Yingtai jumped in. A pair of beautiful butterflies emerged from the grave and flew away happily.

24. THE STORY OF COWHERD AND WEAVING GIRL

Once upon a time, there was a boy named Cowherd (牛郎) because he had no home and lived with his old cow. Early in the morning, Cowherd went to work in the fields and returned home late at night. Meanwhile, there was a lonely weaving girl in the Heavens, who worked endlessly weaving clouds for the Heavenly Queen. Cowherd and Weaving Girl (织女 / 織女) met each other one day, fell in love, and got married. They had two children and lived together very happily. However, the Heavenly Queen was very unhappy with this arrangement, and she sent warriors to capture Weaving Girl and punished the couple by separating them on each side of a big river in the sky, known as the Milky Way. With the help of the old cow and a flock of magpies, Cowherd and Weaving Girl are now able to reunite on a "bridge of magpies" once every year, which happens on the seventh night of the seventh moon. To celebrate their happy reunion, Chinese people refer to this day as China's Valentine's Day.

VOCABULARY INDEX

生词索引
生詞索引

This vocabulary index is arranged in alphabetical order by *pinyin*. Homonyms appear in the order of their tonal pronunciation (i.e., first tones first, second tones second, third tones third, fourth tones fourth, and neutral tones last).

SIMPLIFIED CHARACTERS	TRADITIONAL CHARACTERS	PINYIN	PART OF SPEECH	ENGLISH DEFINITION	STORY NUMBER
A					
爱国(的)	愛國(的)	àiguó (de)	adj.	patriotic	13
安排	安排	ānpái	v.	to arrange	16
安全	安全	ānquán	adj.	safe	3
按照	按照	ànzhào	prep.	according to	1
B					
疤痕	疤痕	bāhén	n.	scar	16
拔下	拔下	báxià	v.	to take off	24
白蛇	白蛇	bái shé	n.	white snake	22
摆手	擺手	bǎishǒu	vo.	to move (one's hands)	10
拜年	拜年	bàinián	v.	to wish somebody a happy New Year	11
宝宝	寶寶	bǎobao	n.	baby	19
抱	抱	bào	v.	to hold	24
背	背	bēi	v.	to carry on the back	6
北	北	běi	n.	north	8

SIMPLIFIED CHARACTERS	TRADITIONAL CHARACTERS	PINYIN	PART OF SPEECH	ENGLISH DEFINITION	STORY NUMBER
本领	本領	běnlǐng	n.	skills	19
毕业	畢業	bìyè	v.	to graduate	23
鞭炮	鞭炮	biānpào	n.	firecracker	11
表达	表達	biǎodá	v.	to express	13
不曾	不曾	bùcéng	adv.	did not (do something)	4
不好意思地	不好意思地	bùhǎo yìsi de	adv.	embarrassedly	1
不久前	不久前	bùjiǔ qián	adv.	a while ago	21
不耐烦	不耐煩	bùnàifán	adj.	impatient	9
不小心	不小心	bùxiǎoxīn	adv.	inadvertently	12
不幸	不幸	bùxìng	adj.	unfortunate	3
布置	布置	bùzhì	v.	to decorate	5
步	步	bù	n.	steps (walking style)	10
c					
才能	才能	cáinéng	n.	talent	9
彩虹	彩虹	cǎihóng	n.	rainbow	23
参观	參觀	cānguān	v.	to visit	18
仓颉	倉頡	Cāng Jié	pn.	(the mythical inventor of Chinese script)	15

SIMPLIFIED CHARACTERS	TRADITIONAL CHARACTERS	PINYIN	PART OF SPEECH	ENGLISH DEFINITION	STORY NUMBER
地(方)	地(方)	dì(fang)	n.	place	4
地震	地震	dìzhèn	n.	earthquake	19
点	點	diǎn	v.	to touch on very briefly (as in painting with a brush)	18
点心	點心	diǎnxin	n.	refreshments	18
雕刻	雕刻	diāokè	v.	to carve	5
掉	掉	diào	v.	to drop, to fall	2
订婚	訂婚	dìnghūn	v.	to be betrothed	21
定为	定為	dìngwéi	vc.	to be decided as	14
丢	丟	diū	v.	to drop	13
洞	洞	dòng	n.	hole	4
抖	抖	dǒu	v.	to shake	19
端午节	端午節	Duānwǔjié	pn.	the Dragon Boat Festival	13
对	對	duì	mw.	pair	23
对方	對方	duìfāng	n.	the other party	24
对联	對聯	duìlián	n.	antithetical couplet	11
躲	躲	duǒ	v.	to hide	3

SIMPLIFIED CHARACTERS	TRADITIONAL CHARACTERS	PINYIN	PART OF SPEECH	ENGLISH DEFINITION	STORY NUMBER
E					
厄运	厄運	èyùn	n.	adversity, misfortune	19
恩爱的	恩愛的	ēn'ài de	adj.	beloved	14
F					
发明	發明	fāmíng	v.	to invent	15
发生	發生	fāshēng	v.	to happen	3
发现	發現	fāxiàn	v.	to discover	15
反而	反而	fǎn'ér	adv.	instead	10
房顶	房頂	fángdǐng	n.	roof	5
房子	房子	fángzi	n.	house	20
放走	放走	fàngzǒu	vc.	to set free	7
飞快地	飛快地	fēikuài de	adv.	swiftly	5
费力地	費力地	fèilì de	adv.	laboriously	9
分成	分成	fēnchéng	vc.	to be divided into	13
分开	分開	fēnkāi	vc.	to separate, to be separated	23
风度	風度	fēngdù	adj./n.	stylish, elegant; demeanor	10
风火轮	風火輪	fēnghuǒ lún	n.	wind-fire wheels	19
丰收	豐收	fēngshōu	n.	abundant harvest	14

SIMPLIFIED CHARACTERS	TRADITIONAL CHARACTERS	PINYIN	PART OF SPEECH	ENGLISH DEFINITION	STORY NUMBER
夫妻	夫妻	fūqī	n.	husband and wife	16
幅	幅	fú	mw.	(measure word for pictures)	18
斧	斧	fǔ	n.	ax, hatchet	2
富人	富人	fùrén	n.	rich person	21

G

赶	趕	gǎn	v.	to drive	8
感动	感動	gǎndòng	v.	to move or be moved, to touch or be touched (emotionally)	6
刚才	剛才	gāngcái	adv.	minutes ago, just now	1
隔壁	隔壁	gébì	n.	next door	4
更加	更加	gèngjiā	adv.	even more	21
姑娘	姑娘	gūniang	n.	girl, lady	20
古代	古代	gǔdài	n.	ancient times	3
固执	固執	gùzhí	adj.	stubborn	6
雇	雇	gù	v.	to hire	8
瓜果	瓜果	guāguǒ	n.	vegetables and fruits	14
刮起	颳起	guāqǐ	vc.	to start blowing sharply (as a wind)	22

SIMPLIFIED CHARACTERS	TRADITIONAL CHARACTERS	PINYIN	PART OF SPEECH	ENGLISH DEFINITION	STORY NUMBER
关	關	guān	v.	to imprison	22
关于	關於	guānyú	prep.	about, concerning	12
观察	觀察	guānchá	v.	to observe	2
观音娘娘	觀音娘娘	Guānyīn Niángniang	pn.	Bodhisattva Guanyin	21
过年	過年	guònián	v.	to celebrate Chinese New Year	11
H					
害怕	害怕	hàipà	v.	to be afraid of	3
害人	害人	hàirén	v.o.	to hurt people	11
旱	旱	hàn	n.	drought	14
好	好	hào	v.	to love, to favor	5
和尚	和尚	héshàng	n.	Buddhist monk	18
合上	合上	héshang	vc.	to (be) shut	23
轰	轟	hōng	on.	bang, boom	18
红包	红包	hóngbāo	n.	red envelope	11
猴(子)	猴(子)	hóu(zi)	n.	monkey	17
厚	厚	hòu	adj.	thick	16
后羿	后羿	Hòu Yì	pn.	(name of a person)	14

SIMPLIFIED CHARACTERS	TRADITIONAL CHARACTERS	PINYIN	PART OF SPEECH	ENGLISH DEFINITION	STORY NUMBER
忽然	忽然	hūrán	adv.	suddenly	1
狐(狸)	狐(狸)	hú(li)	n.	fox	7
湖边	湖邊	húbiān	n.	lakeside, beside the lake	21
蝴蝶	蝴蝶	húdié	n.	butterfly	23
(老)虎	(老)虎	(lǎo)hǔ	n.	tiger	7
互相	互相	hùxiāng	adv.	each other, mutually	16
花轿	花轎	huājiào	n.	bridal sedan chair	23
划	划	huá	v.	to row (a boat)	13
划	劃	huà	v.	to slash	24
画龙	畫龍	huà lóng	vo.	to paint a dragon	18
画家	畫家	huàjiā	n.	artist, painter	18
(怀)疑	(懷)疑	(huái)yí	v./n.	to suspect; doubt	2
怀孕	懷孕	huáiyùn	v.	to be pregnant	22
慌张	慌張	huāngzhāng	adj.	nervous	2
黄帝	黃帝	Huángdì	pn.	the Yellow Emperor	15
皇家考试	皇家考試	huángjiā kǎoshì	n.	Imperial Examination	21
回答	回答	huídá	v.	to answer	6

SIMPLIFIED CHARACTERS	TRADITIONAL CHARACTERS	PINYIN	PART OF SPEECH	ENGLISH DEFINITION	STORY NUMBER
婚姻	婚姻	hūnyīn	n.	marriage	16
混天绫	混天綾	hùn tiān líng	n.	celestial red silk sash	19

J

SIMPLIFIED CHARACTERS	TRADITIONAL CHARACTERS	PINYIN	PART OF SPEECH	ENGLISH DEFINITION	STORY NUMBER
鸡	雞	jī	n.	chicken	15
吉祥	吉祥	jíxiáng	adj.	auspicious	11
集市	集市	jíshì	n.	marketplace	1
挤满	擠滿	jǐmǎn	vc.	to be crowded	10
挤破	擠破	jǐpò	vc.	to break	5
记录	記錄	jìlù	v.	to record	15
纪念	紀念	jìniàn	v.	to commemorate	12
技术	技術	jìshù	n.	skill	8
袈裟	袈裟	jiāshā	n.	*Kasaya* (vestment) for a Buddhist monk	22
假	假	jiǎ	v./adj.	to pretend to (be/have); false	7, 21
架	架	jià	v.	to build	24
剑	劍	jiàn	n.	sword	19
狡猾	狡猾	jiǎohuá	adj.	sly, cunning	7
脚印	腳印	jiǎoyìn	n.	footprint	15

SIMPLIFIED CHARACTERS	TRADITIONAL CHARACTERS	PINYIN	PART OF SPEECH	ENGLISH DEFINITION	STORY NUMBER
节日	節日	jiérì	n.	holiday	11
结	結	jié	n.	knot	15
结束	結束	jiéshù	v.	to end	11
解决	解決	jiějué	v.	to solve	19
金簪	金簪	jīnzān	n.	gold hairpin	24
紧紧地	緊緊地	jǐnjǐn de	adv.	tightly	17
进行	進行	jìnxíng	v.	to carry out	13
睛	睛	jīng	n.	eyes	18
精	精	jīng	n.	spirit	21
经过	經過	jīngguò	v.	to pass by	23
惊醒	驚醒	jīngxǐng	v.	to wake with a start	5
决定	決定	juédìng	v.	to decide	4

K

砍柴	砍柴	kǎnchái	vo.	to cut wood	2
烤干	烤乾	kǎogān	vc.	to roast dry	14
靠在	靠在	kàozài	v.	to lean on	9
渴	渴	kě	adj.	thirsty	14

SIMPLIFIED CHARACTERS	TRADITIONAL CHARACTERS	PINYIN	PART OF SPEECH	ENGLISH DEFINITION	STORY NUMBER
可怜	可憐	kělián	adj.	pitiful	3
可惜	可惜	kěxī	adj.	pitiful, unfortunate	9
可笑	可笑	kěxiào	adj.	absurd, ridiculous	3
客气地	客氣地	kèqi de	adv.	politely	16
口袋	口袋	kǒudài	n.	pocket	16
宽	寬	kuān	adj.	wide	24
困难	困難	kùnnan	adj.	difficult	21
L					
拉	拉	lā	v.	to pull	24
蜡烛	蠟燭	làzhú	n.	candle	12
拦	攔	lán	v.	to stop, to hinder, to block	22
浪费	浪費	làngfèi	adj.	wasteful	9
雷电交加	雷電交加	léidiàn jiāojiā	ce.	thunder and lightning	23
泪水	淚水	lèishuǐ	n.	tears	24
冷冷地	冷冷地	lěnglěng de	adv.	coldly	21
愣住	愣住	lèngzhù	v.	to stun or be stunned	7

SIMPLIFIED CHARACTERS	TRADITIONAL CHARACTERS	PINYIN	PART OF SPEECH	ENGLISH DEFINITION	STORY NUMBER
离开	離開	líkāi	vc.	to depart from	14
李靖	李靖	Lǐ Jìng	pn.	(name of a person)	19
鲤鱼	鯉魚	lǐyú	n.	carp	21
历法	歷法	lìfǎ	n.	calendar	11
力量	力量	lìliang	n.	strength	19
力气	力氣	lìqi	n.	strength	6
连着	連著	liánzhe	v.	to be continuous	20
脸红	臉紅	liǎnhóng	vc.	to blush	24
两	兩	liǎng	mw.	(measure word for silver)	4
亮闪闪的	亮閃閃的	liàngshǎnshǎn de	adj.	shining	19
了不起	了不起	liǎobùqǐ	adj.	amazing, terrific	7
劣	劣	liè	adj.	inferior, bad	9
猎人	獵人	lièrén	n.	hunter	15
邻(居)	鄰(居)	lín(jū)	n.	neighbor	2
淋湿	淋濕	línshī	v.	to drench	22

SIMPLIFIED CHARACTERS	TRADITIONAL CHARACTERS	PINYIN	PART OF SPEECH	ENGLISH DEFINITION	STORY NUMBER
流传	流傳	liúchuán	v.	to circulate, to spread	19
流放	流放	liúfàng	v.	to exile	13
漏	漏	lòu	v.	to leak	21
路费	路費	lùfèi	n.	travel expenses	8
履	履	lǚ	n.	shoes	1
旅店	旅店	lǚdiàn	n.	hotel, inn	10
旅费	旅費	lǚfèi	n.	travel expenses	10

M

SIMPLIFIED CHARACTERS	TRADITIONAL CHARACTERS	PINYIN	PART OF SPEECH	ENGLISH DEFINITION	STORY NUMBER
马车夫	馬車夫	mǎchēfū	n.	cart/wagon driver	8
骂	罵	mà	v.	to scold, to berate	19
埋	埋	mái	v.	to bury	4
迈步	邁步	màibù	vo.	to step forward	10
满不在乎	滿不在乎	mǎnbù zàihu	adj.	giving no heed	8
满满的	滿滿的	mǎnmǎn de	adj.	full	9
满足	滿足	mǎnzú	v.	to satisfy	5
慢慢地	慢慢地	mànmàn de	adv.	slowly	4
眉毛	眉毛	méimao	n.	brow	16

SIMPLIFIED CHARACTERS	TRADITIONAL CHARACTERS	PINYIN	PART OF SPEECH	ENGLISH DEFINITION	STORY NUMBER
美满	美滿	měimǎn	adj.	happy and fulfilled	11
蒙着脸	蒙著臉	méngzhe liǎn	vo.	to be masked	24
梦	夢	mèng	n.	dream	11
迷路	迷路	mílù	vo.	to get lost	12
汨罗江	汨羅江	Mìluójiāng	pn.	(name of a river)	13
面	面	miàn	mw.	(measure word for wall)	4
明白	明白	míngbai	v.	to understand, to realize	18
命运	命運	mìngyùn	n.	destiny	13
模仿	模仿	mófǎng	v.	to imitate	10
墓	墓	mù	n.	grave	23

N

SIMPLIFIED CHARACTERS	TRADITIONAL CHARACTERS	PINYIN	PART OF SPEECH	ENGLISH DEFINITION	STORY NUMBER
南	南	nán	n.	south	8
南天门	南天門	Nántiānmén	pn.	the Southern Heavenly Gate	17
难得的	難得的	nándé de	adj.	rare, hard to come by	9
闹海	鬧海	nào hǎi	vo.	to fight dragons in the sea	19
年糕	年糕	niángāo	n.	rice cake (for the New Year)	11
年关	年關	niánguān	n.	end of the year	11

SIMPLIFIED CHARACTERS	TRADITIONAL CHARACTERS	PINYIN	PART OF SPEECH	ENGLISH DEFINITION	STORY NUMBER
年轻	年輕	niánqīng	adj.	young	6
宁死	寧死	nìngsǐ	v.	to rather die	13
牛角	牛角	niújiǎo	n.	ox horn	17
牛郎	牛郎	Niúláng	pn.	Cowherd	24
农历	農歷	nónglì	n.	lunar calendar	11
农作物	農作物	nóngzuòwù	n.	crops	14
弄坏	弄壞	nònghuài	vc.	to damage	19

P

啪	啪	pā	on.	(sound of popping or bursting)	19
拍	拍	pāi	v.	to pat	9
派	派	pài	v.	to dispatch	6
抛弃	抛棄	pāoqì	v.	to abandon	21
咆哮	咆哮	páoxiào	v.	to roar, to thunder	19
披	披	pī	v.	to drape over the shoulders	9
骗	騙	piàn	v.	to lie, to deceive	18
平平安安	平平安安	píngpíng 'ān'ān	adj.	peaceful and safe	11

SIMPLIFIED CHARACTERS	TRADITIONAL CHARACTERS	PINYIN	PART OF SPEECH	ENGLISH DEFINITION	STORY NUMBER
Q					
骑	騎	qí	v.	to mount	24
杞(国)人	杞(國)人	Qǐ(guó)rén	n.	a person from the state of Qi	3
乾坤圈	乾坤圈	qiánkūn quān	n.	universe ring	19
强壮	強壯	qiáng zhuàng	adj.	strong	7
强迫	強迫	qiǎngpò	v.	to force	10
悄悄地	悄悄地	qiāoqiāo de	adv.	secretly	2
桥	橋	qiáo	n.	bridge	24
秦国	秦國	Qínguó	pn.	the state of Qin	13
轻快	輕快	qīngkuài	adj.	light and fast	10
轻飘飘的	輕飄飄的	qīng piāopiāo de	adj.	buoyant	14
轻轻地	輕輕地	qīngqīng de	adv.	gently, lightly	9
轻易地	輕易地	qīngyì de	adv.	easily	18
情人节	情人節	Qíngrénjié	pn.	Valentine's Day	24
求婚	求婚	qiúhūn	vo.	to propose marriage	23
劝告	勸告	quàngào	n.	advice	8
缺	缺	quē	adj.	fragmented	12
却	卻	què	conj.	but, however	8

SIMPLIFIED CHARACTERS	TRADITIONAL CHARACTERS	PINYIN	PART OF SPEECH	ENGLISH DEFINITION	STORY NUMBER
R					
热爱	熱愛	rè'ài	v.	to love passionately	13
热气腾腾	熱氣騰騰	rèqì téngténg	adj.	piping hot	20
人间	人間	rénjiān	n.	the human world	12
人物	人物	rénwù	n.	people, figures	18
S					
撒野	撒野	sāyě	v.	to act wildly	19
洒下来	灑下來	sǎ xiàlai	vc.	to pour down (as light, water, etc.)	14
伞	傘	sǎn	n.	umbrella	22
散	散	sàn	v.	to disperse, to scatter	1
森林	森林	sēnlín	n.	forest	7
杀	殺	shā	v.	to kill	19
傻事	傻事	shǎshì	np.	silly things	6
伤害	傷害	shānghài	v.	to harm	13
烧死	燒死	shāosǐ	vc.	to burn to death	12
烧香	燒香	shāoxiāng	vo.	to burn incense	22
蛇精	蛇精	shéjīng	n.	snake spirit	22

SIMPLIFIED CHARACTERS	TRADITIONAL CHARACTERS	PINYIN	PART OF SPEECH	ENGLISH DEFINITION	STORY NUMBER
射	射	shè	v.	to shoot down	12
设置	設置	shèzhì	v.	to design, to arrange	12
神鸟	神鳥	shénniǎo	n.	celestial bird, phoenix	12
神气	神氣	shénqì	adj.	cocky	7
神仙	神仙	shénxiān	n.	immortal, supernatural being	6
生肖	生肖	shēngxiào	n.	any of the twelve zodiac animals	17
声音	聲音	shēngyīn	n.	sound, noise	4
剩下	剩下	shèngxià	vc.	to be left over	18
诗人	詩人	shīrén	n.	poet	13
失望	失望	shīwàng	adj.	disappointed	10
识(别)	識(別)	shí(bié)	v.	to distinguish	9
世界	世界	shìjiè	n.	world	5
收获	收獲	shōuhuò	v.	to harvest	14
收拾	收拾	shōushi	v.	to clean up	20
首领	首領	shǒulǐng	n.	chief, leader	15
守岁	守歲	shǒusuì	v.	to keep awake to see the New Year in	11
瘦	瘦	shòu	adj.	skinny, thin	9

SIMPLIFIED CHARACTERS	TRADITIONAL CHARACTERS	PINYIN	PART OF SPEECH	ENGLISH DEFINITION	STORY NUMBER
书生	書生	shūshēng	n.	student, scholar	20
(老)鼠	(老)鼠	(lǎo)shǔ	n.	rat, mouse	17
树丛	樹叢	shùcóng	n.	bushes, thicket	7
甩尾巴	甩尾巴	shuǎi wěiba	vo.	to swing one's tail	18
拴住	拴住	shuānzhù	vc.	to fasten	16
寺	寺	sì	n.	temple	22
寺庙	寺廟	sìmiào	n.	temple	18
所有	所有	suǒyǒu	adj.	all	7
T					
踏	踏	tà	v.	to step on	19
太乙真人	太乙真人	Tàiyǐ Zhēnrén	pn.	(name of a Daoist immortal)	19
弹琴	彈琴	tán qín	vo.	to play a stringed musical instrument	23
汤圆	湯圓	tāngyuán	n.	sweet dumpling	11
逃	逃	táo	v.	to escape	22
逃走	逃走	táozǒu	vc.	to escape	7
特征	特徵	tèzhēng	n.	characteristics, features	15
天兵天将	天兵天將	tiānbīng tiānjiàng	n.	heavenly warriors	24

SIMPLIFIED CHARACTERS	TRADITIONAL CHARACTERS	PINYIN	PART OF SPEECH	ENGLISH DEFINITION	STORY NUMBER
天帝	天帝	Tiāndì	pn.	Heavenly God	12
甜	甜	tián	adj.	sweet	11
挑	挑	tiāo	v.	to select, to choose; to carry on the shoulder	1, 6
同情	同情	tóngqíng	v.	to sympathize	14
痛苦	痛苦	tòngkǔ	adj.	painful, sad	13
头	頭	tóu	mw.	(measure word for big animals)	24
投江	投江	tóujiāng	vo.	to jump into a river	13
突然	突然	tūrán	adv.	suddenly	15
图案	圖案	tú'àn	n.	pattern	5
图形	圖形	túxíng	n.	patterns	15
团聚	團聚	tuánjù	v.	to be reunited	24
团团圆圆	團團圓圓	tuántuán yuányuán	adj.	(family) reunion	11
脱下	脫下	tuōxià	vc.	to take off	9, 22

W

SIMPLIFIED CHARACTERS	TRADITIONAL CHARACTERS	PINYIN	PART OF SPEECH	ENGLISH DEFINITION	STORY NUMBER
挖	挖	wā	v.	to dig	4
王母娘娘	王母娘娘	Wángmǔ Niángniang	pn.	the Heavenly Queen	14

SIMPLIFIED CHARACTERS	TRADITIONAL CHARACTERS	PINYIN	PART OF SPEECH	ENGLISH DEFINITION	STORY NUMBER
望	望	wàng	v.	to stare at	24
忘记	忘記	wàngjì	v.	to forget	1
威风	威風	wēifēng	adj.	powerful, imposing	7
威(力)	威(力)	wēi(lì)	n.	power	7
韦固	韋固	Wéi Gù	pn.	(name of a person)	16
为难	為難	wéinán	v.	to feel awkward	17
为生	為生	wéishēng	v.	to make a living	2
尾巴	尾巴	wěiba	n.	tail	9
伟大的	偉大的	wěidà de	adj.	great	13
魏国	魏國	Wèiguó	pn.	the state of Wei	8
屋顶	屋頂	wūdǐng	n.	roof	19
无	無	wú	v.	to not have, to be without	4

X

牺牲	犧牲	xīshēng	v.	to sacrifice	19
习惯	習慣	xíguàn	n.	habit, custom	10
喜鹊	喜鵲	xǐquè	n.	magpie	24
喜悦	喜悅	xǐyuè	n.	happiness	14

SIMPLIFIED CHARACTERS	TRADITIONAL CHARACTERS	PINYIN	PART OF SPEECH	ENGLISH DEFINITION	STORY NUMBER
细	細	xì	adj.	slim	15
吓呆	嚇呆	xiàdāi	vc.	to be scared stiff	18
下决心	下決心	xiàjuéxīn	vo.	to make up one's mind	15
仙草	仙草	xiāncǎo	n.	celestial herbs	22
先后顺序	先後順序	xiānhòu shùnxù	n.	order of sequencing	17
仙女	仙女	xiānnǚ	n.	fairy maiden	20
仙药	仙藥	xiānyào	n.	celestial elixir	14
显示	顯示	xiǎnshì	v.	to show, to demonstrate	7
羡慕	羨慕	xiànmù	v.	to envy	23
相信	相信	xiāngxìn	v.	to believe	16
想念	想念	xiǎngniàn	v.	to miss	14
消息	消息	xiāoxi	n.	news	12
小声地	小聲地	xiǎoshēng de	adv.	softly (in tone), quietly	20
新娘子	新娘子	xīnniángzi	n.	bride	23
幸亏	幸虧	xìngkuī	adv.	fortunately	16
凶恶	凶惡	xiōng'è	adj.	fierce, ferocious	11
修炼	修煉	xiūliàn	v.	to practice asceticism	22

SIMPLIFIED CHARACTERS	TRADITIONAL CHARACTERS	PINYIN	PART OF SPEECH	ENGLISH DEFINITION	STORY NUMBER
Y					
压岁钱	壓歲錢	yāsùiqián	n.	money given for good luck in the New Year	11
烟花	煙花	yānhuā	n.	fireworks	12
燕国	燕國	Yānguó	pn.	the state of Yan	10
羊	羊	yáng	n.	goat, sheep	17
养父	養父	yǎngfù	n.	foster father	16
妖怪	妖怪	yāoguài	n.	monster	11
摇摇晃晃	搖搖晃晃	yáoyáo huàng huàng	v.	to tremble	19
叶公	葉公	Yè Gōng	pn.	(name of a person)	5
一模一样	一模一樣	yīmú yīyàng	adj.	exactly the same	21
移	移	yí	v.	to move away	6
以为	以為	yǐwéi	v.	to believe (incorrectly)	12
意见	意見	yìjiàn	n.	idea, opinion	13
意思	意思	yìsi	n.	meaning	4
银(子)	銀(子)	yín(zi)	n.	silver, money	4
银河	銀河	Yínhé	pn.	Milky Way	24

SIMPLIFIED CHARACTERS	TRADITIONAL CHARACTERS	PINYIN	PART OF SPEECH	ENGLISH DEFINITION	STORY NUMBER
应该	應該	yīnggāi	av.	should	4
迎接	迎接	yíngjiē	v.	to welcome	11
忧	憂	yōu	v.	to fear, to worry about	3
优美	優美	yōuměi	adj.	graceful	10
游戏	遊戲	yóuxì	n.	game	11
友好	友好	yǒuhǎo	adj.	friendly	24
鱼	魚	yú	n.	fish	15
愚公	愚公	Yú Gōng	pn.	(name of a person [lit. Foolish Old Man])	6
遇到	遇到	yùdào	vc.	to encounter	22
玉帝	玉帝	Yùdì	pn.	the Jade Emperor	17
玉皇大帝	玉皇大帝	Yùhuáng Dàdì	pn.	the Jade Emperor	6
遇见	遇見	yùjiàn	v.	to meet, to encounter	16
辕	轅	yuán	n.	shafts of a wagon	8
原来	原來	yuánlái	ce.	it turned out to be	2
原谅	原諒	yuánliàng	v.	to forgive	19
元宵节	元宵節	Yuánxiāojié	pn.	the Lantern Festival	12

SIMPLIFIED CHARACTERS	TRADITIONAL CHARACTERS	PINYIN	PART OF SPEECH	ENGLISH DEFINITION	STORY NUMBER
愿望	願望	yuànwàng	n.	wish	4
院子	院子	yuànzi	n.	yard	4
月饼	月餅	yuèbǐng	n.	moon cake	14
月宫	月宫	yuègōng	n.	Moon Palace	14
月亮	月亮	yuèliang	n.	moon	3
运气	運氣	yùnqi	n.	luck, fortune	11
运输	運輸	yùnshū	v.	to transport	9

Z

SIMPLIFIED CHARACTERS	TRADITIONAL CHARACTERS	PINYIN	PART OF SPEECH	ENGLISH DEFINITION	STORY NUMBER
灾难	災難	zāinàn	n.	disaster	12
造字	造字	zàozì	vo.	to coin new Chinese characters	15
战胜	戰勝	zhànshèng	vc.	to triumph over	12
张僧繇	張僧繇	Zhāng Sēngyáo	pn.	(name of a person)	18
照顾	照顧	zhàogù	v.	to take care of	9
召集	召集	zhàojí	v.	to summon	15
遮雨	遮雨	zhēyǔ	vo.	to keep out the rain	22
辙	轍	zhé	n.	wheel ruts of a wagon	8
珍惜	珍惜	zhēnxī	v.	to cherish	14

SIMPLIFIED CHARACTERS	TRADITIONAL CHARACTERS	PINYIN	PART OF SPEECH	ENGLISH DEFINITION	STORY NUMBER
整整齐齐地	整整齊齊地	zhěngzhěng qiqi de	adv.	neatly	20
正常的	正常的	zhèngcháng de	adj.	normal	14
证据	證據	zhèngjù	n.	evidence	2
郑(国)人	鄭(國)人	Zhèng(guó) rén	n.	a person from the state of Zheng	1
织布	織布	zhībù	vo.	to weave cloth	24
织女	織女	Zhīnǚ	pn.	Weaving Girl	24
之一	之一	zhīyī	n.	one of	12
指	指	zhǐ	v.	to point at	21
智叟	智叟	Zhì Sǒu	pn.	(name of a person [lit. Smart Old Man])	6
终点	終點	zhōngdiǎn	n.	destination	17
周围	周圍	zhōuwéi	n.	surroundings	15
咒语	咒語	zhòuyǔ	n.	curse	19
竹叶	竹葉	zhúyè	n.	bamboo leaves	13
注定	注定	zhùdìng	vc.	to decide by fate	16
柱子	柱子	zhùzi	n.	pillar	5
抓走	抓走	zhuāzǒu	vc.	to arrest	13

SIMPLIFIED CHARACTERS	TRADITIONAL CHARACTERS	PINYIN	PART OF SPEECH	ENGLISH DEFINITION	STORY NUMBER
传	傳	zhuàn	n.	legend, story	22
赚	賺	zhuàn	v.	to earn	4
追不上	追不上	zhuībùshàng	vc.	to be unable to catch up	8
准备	准備	zhǔnbèi	n.	preparation	12
姿势	姿勢	zīshì	n.	posture	10
自杀	自殺	zìshā	v.	to commit suicide	19
粽子	粽子	zòngzi	n.	sticky rice wrapped in bamboo leaves	13
组合	組合	zǔhé	vc.	to compose	15
作用	作用	zuòyòng	n.	role	9

ANSWER KEY (Reading Comprehension)

Story 1

1. B
2. B
3. C
4. D
5. B
6. D
7. C

Story 2

1. C
2. B
3. C
4. A
5. D
6. A
7. B

Story 3

1. D
2. D
3. C
4. B
5. A
6. D
7. A

Story 4

1. B
2. D
3. C
4. A
5. C
6. D
7. D

Story 5

1. D
2. C
3. D
4. C
5. B
6. A
7. C

Story 6

1. B
2. C
3. B
4. D
5. B

Story 7

1. B
2. C
3. A
4. D
5. C
6. A
7. C

Story 8

1. C
2. D
3. B
4. A
5. D

Story 9

1. C
2. D
3. B
4. A
5. C
6. A
7. C

Story 10

1. C
2. D
3. A
4. B
5. A

Story 11

1. D
2. B
3. B
4. D
5. C
6. C
7. D

Story 12

1. C
2. A
3. C
4. D
5. B

Story 13

1. D
2. B
3. C
4. B
5. C
6. B
7. A

Story 14

1. D
2. C
3. B
4. C
5. A

Story 15

1. B
2. D
3. A
4. C
5. C

Story 16

1. A
2. C
3. D
4. A
5. B

Story 17

1. B
2. A
3. C
4. C
5. D
6. D
7. B

Story 18

1. A
2. B
3. B
4. D
5. C

Story 19

1. B
2. C
3. D
4. B
5. C
6. A
7. D

Story 20

1. B
2. A
3. D
4. C
5. A
6. C
7. B

Story 21

1. A
2. C
3. C
4. B
5. A
6. D
7. C

Story 22

1. B
2. C
3. D
4. B
5. C
6. A
7. C

Story 23

1. C
2. B
3. A
4. B
5. D
6. C
7. C

Story 24

1. B
2. A
3. B
4. D
5. C
6. A
7. B

ABOUT THE AUTHORS

Yun Xiao is Professor of Chinese Language and Linguistics at Bryant University. She has a Ph.D. degree in linguistics. Her research interests are second language acquisition and pedagogy, Chinese syntax and discourse analysis, and Chinese teacher education. Her recent publications include more than twenty articles and book chapters. She is the primary author of *Tales and Traditions* (Volumes 1–4); and co-editor of *Teaching Chinese as a Foreign Language: Theories and Applications*.

Ying Wang is a Visiting Instructor of Chinese at Wheaton College. She obtained her M.A. from the Department of Asian Languages and Literatures at the University of Massachusetts Amherst and her B.A. in Chinese Language and Literature from Beijing University. She has taught at the Central Broadcasting and TV University in Beijing. Her areas of interest include classical Chinese literature; the history of Chinese writing; and the development, simplification, and standardization of Chinese characters. She is the author of multiple works on classical Chinese literature and a translator of children's stories.

Hui Faye Xiao is Associate Professor in the Department of East Asian Languages and Cultures at the University of Kansas. Her recent publications have appeared in *Chinese Literature Today, Modern Chinese Literature and Culture* (MCLC), *Journal of Chinese Cinemas, Journal of Contemporary China, Chinese Films in Focus II,* and *Gender and Modernity in Global Youth Cultures*. She is a co-author of Volumes 1, 2, and 4 of *Tales and Traditions*.

Wenjie Liu holds a B.A. in Chinese Language and Literature and an M.A. in Sociology from Nanjing University, China. She received a second M.A. in Chinese Language and Literature from the University of Massachusetts Amherst. Her research interests are in classical Chinese prose, late-Ming literature, and teaching Chinese as a second language.

FOR FURTHER STUDY

More Readers Published by Cheng & Tsui

Readings in Chinese Culture Series, Volumes 1–5
By Weijia Huang, Qun Ao

Increase reading and cultural proficiency with original, level-appropriate essays about ancient and contemporary Chinese culture.

1: The Sky Is Bright with Stars	978-0-88727-818-1
2: How Far Away Is the Sun?	978-0-88727-535-7
3: The Moon Is Always Beautiful	978-0-88727-637-8
4: Where Does the Wind Blow?	978-0-88727-881-5
5: Watching the Clouds Go By	978-1-62291-055-7

Chinese Biographies Series, Second Edition
By Grace Wu

Readings in natural, authentic language chronicle the lives of modern-day, Chinese-speaking pop culture icons. Available in simplified characters.

	With *pinyin* annotations	Without *pinyin* annotations
Lang Lang	978-1-62291-098-4	978-1-62291-100-4
Yao Ming	978-1-62291-097-7	978-1-62291-099-1
Jay Chou	978-1-62291-109-7	978-1-62291-110-3
Jeremy Lin	978-1-62291-111-0	978-1-62291-112-7
Ang Lee	978-1-62291-113-4	978-1-62291-114-1
Vera Wang	978-1-62291-107-3	978-1-62291-108-0

Reference Texts Published by Cheng & Tsui

The Way of Chinese Characters, Second Edition
The Origins of 670 Essential Words
漢字之道
By Jianhsin Wu, Illustrated by Chen Zheng and Chen Tian

Enrich character study with cultural insight, linguistic context, and playful illustrations.

978-1-62291-046-5

Cheng & Tsui Chinese Character Dictionary
A Guide to the 2000 Most Frequently-Used Characters
剑桥学生写字字典
Edited by Wang Huidi

Carry this pocket-sized guide of 2,000 core characters organized alphabetically by *pinyin* to reference stroke orders, basic meaning, and examples of use.

978-0-88727-314-8